It's another Quality Book from CGP

This book is for anyone doing GCSE Geography.

It contains lots of tricky questions designed to make you sweat — because that's the only way you'll get any better.

It's also got some daft bits in to try and make the whole experience at least vaguely entertaining for you.

What CGP is all about

Our sole aim here at CGP is to produce the highest quality books — carefully written, immaculately presented and dangerously close to being funny.

Then we work our socks off to get them out to you — at the cheapest possible prices.

Contents

Section One — Population

Population 1
Population Density 2
Population Growth 4
Population Structure 6
Population Structure and Dependency 8
Managing Population Growth 9
Migration 11
Types of Migration 12

Section Two — Settlement

Houses and Stuff 14
The Settlement Hierachy 15
The Sphere of Influence of a Settlement 16
Urban Land Use in MEDC Cities 18
Urbanisation 20
Counterurbanisation 21
Problems in MEDC Cities 22
Urban Problems of LEDCs 24
Planning and the Rural-Urban Fringe 26

Section Three — Farming

Farming 27
Classifying Farming 28
Distribution of Farming Types 30
Farming in the EU — Economics and Politics 31
Modern Farming in MEDCs 33
Farming in LEDCs 34
The Green Revolution 36
Farming and the Environment 38

Section Four — Industry

The Classification of Industry	40
The Location of Industry	42
Industry in LEDCs	45
The NICs	46
Changing Industry – MEDCs	48
Multinational Companies	50

Section Five — Managing Resources

Use and Abuse of Resources	51
Energy and Power	53
Acid Rain	55
Global Warming	56
Pollution	58
National Parks	60
Tourism and Conflict	62
Tourism in LEDCs	64

Section Six — Development

Measuring Development	65
Contrasts in Development	66
Environmental Problems and Development	68
Dependency and the Colonial Past	69
International Trade	70
The Question of Aid	73
Development Projects	75

Section Seven — Answers 76

Published by Coordination Group Publications Ltd.
Additional Illustrations by: Lex Ward

Contributors:
Charley Darbishire
Chris Dennett
Dominic Hall
Andy Park
Claire Thompson
James Paul Wallis
Eileen Worthington
Suzanne Worthington

With Thanks to:
Magda Halsall for the proofreading.

ISBN: 978 1 84146 701 6

Groovy website: www.cgpbooks.co.uk
Jolly bits of clipart from CorelDRAW®
Printed by Elanders Hindson Ltd, Newcastle upon Tyne.

Text, design, layout and original illustrations © Coordination Group Publications Ltd. 2001
All rights reserved.

Section One — Population

Population

Welcome to human geography. Straight off, we're talking <u>people</u> — <u>where</u> they live, and <u>why</u> they live there. Enjoy.

Q1. Write a definition of "Population Distribution".

....
....
....

Q2. In the following list, circle the four areas which have large populations.

Greenland;   The Moon;   Japan;   Bangladesh;   Amazonia;

North Western Europe;   Eastern USA;   The Australian Outback.

Q3. Make <u>two</u> lists by writing these statements under the correct headings.

Their climate is not extreme. They are desert areas. They are high mountainous areas. They are very cold areas. They are lowland areas. They are rich industrial areas. They are poor areas of rapid population growth. They are areas of fertile soils.

Reasons why areas have many people	Reasons why areas have few people
....	....
....	....
....	....
....	....
....	....

Q4. Match up each of these areas with a reason for its large or small population. The first one is done for you.

Sahara desert — small population because it's very cold and windy with dark winters

Europe — small population because it's too steep and cold for buildings and crops

North Canada — small population because it's very hot and dry making farming difficult

Bangladesh — large population because it's a wealthy industrial area

The Himalayas — large population because it's fertile lowland with rapid population growth

People — don't you just luv 'em?...

Population distribution — just common sense really. A lot of human geography's like this. Obviously you'll get more people where it's nice to live, but for the <u>exam</u> you need to know all the picky reasons. Practice makes perfect — that's what these questions are for. Get practising.

Section One — Population

Population Density

You need to know population density for one of two reasons — either you're Mr Spod the town planner, or you want to pass a <u>geography exam</u>. I'll give you two guesses.

Q1. Write a definition of "Population Density".

   ....

   ....

   ....

Q2. Complete the formula for working out the population density:

   Population Density = <u>Number of people</u>
   ....

Q3. What's the difference between population <u>distribution</u> and population <u>density</u>?

   ....

   ....

   ....

Q4. Answer these questions about Bangladesh, which has too many people compared to the available resources.

   a) What is the correct word for this problem? O............................

   b) In this list, circle <u>five</u> examples of the "resources" that are lacking.

   File paper;   food;   clean water;   videos;   soil;   paint;   oil and gas;   houses.

   c) Describe <u>one</u> fact about Bangladesh that shows the country has too many people to cope with.

   ....

   ....

Q5. Describe what is meant by "underpopulation" and name an example.

   ....

   ....

Q6. Fill in the blanks to complete this sentence.

   The .... is the ideal number of people for the resources available.

Section One — Population

Population Density

Q7. Look at the map and answer the questions:

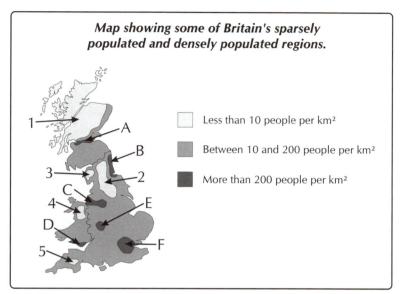

a) Do most people live in the north and west or the south and east?
   ....

b) Name the sparsely populated areas, 1 to 5.

   1. .... 2. .... 3. ....

   4. .... 5. ....

c) Are the areas in b) remote areas with few jobs or wealthy areas with high employment?
   ....

d) Identify the densely populated areas shown on the map by finishing off these descriptions:

   A The Central Lowlands of .... including

      the cities of G .... and E ....

   B The industrial areas of North East England, including the city of .... upon Tyne.

   C The industrial areas of North West England, including the

      cities of L ...., and M ....

   D South Wales, where industry grew up based on c .... mining.

   E The industrial area of the M ....

   F The wealthy area around L ....

Geography — it is your density... I mean, destiny...

The world's rising population is an important issue nowadays — and that's one of the reasons why it always comes up in exams. I guess because of the usual rubbish about being able to 'apply your knowledge' etc. When all they really want you to do is learn the facts...

Section One — Population

Population Growth

"I remember when this was all fields..." Everyone (even grandma) knows there are more and more people and they're spreading everywhere. You need to know <u>how many</u> more, and <u>why</u>.

Q1. Look at the graph of world population growth and answer the questions which follow:

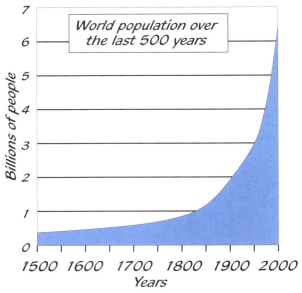

a) What was the population of the world in the year 1500? ....

b) What was the population of the world in the year 1800? ....

c) So in 17 centuries (from year 1500 to 1800), had it increased ×2, ×4 or ×6? ....

d) What was the world population in 2000? ....

e) So in 3 centuries (from 1800 to 2000), had it increased roughly ×2, ×4, ×6, or ×8? ....

f) Write a conclusion about the rates of increase of the world population.

....

....

Q2. Answer these questions about the <u>three</u> variables which affect population growth.

a) Give a definition of the first variable — <u>birth rate</u>.

....

....

b) Give a definition of the second variable — <u>death rate</u>.

....

....

c) What is the third variable?

....

Section One — Population

Population Growth

Q3. Circle the correct answer to this question: In the last few hundred years, the world's population has grown very rapidly — what do we call this?

    The Big Bang Theory   The Population Explosion

Q4. What is the name for the diagram that shows the four stages of change in a population? ....

Q5. Look at the diagram of changes in Britain's population and answer the questions which follow.

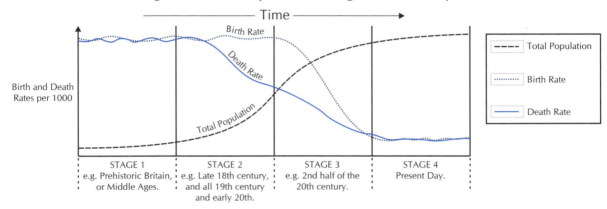

a) Circle the reason why birth rates were high in stage 1.

    No birth control   People could afford to have lots of children

b) Circle the reason why the death rate was high in stage 1.

    Road accidents   Disease, wars and starvation

c) What happened to the death rate in stage 2, and why?

....

....

d) What happened to the rate of population growth in stage 2?

....

....

e) Are birth and death rates low or high today (stage 4)? ....

f) What has this done to the rate of population growth?

....

So many people — the storks must be exhausted...

Growing populations are a real pain. You need more roads, and more schools, and more hospitals, and more... Never mind, for these questions you just need to know the <u>numbers</u> and the <u>reasons</u>. It's a bit gruesome putting the whole glory of life down to <u>births</u> and <u>deaths</u>, but there you go.

Population Structure

Population structure. No, it's nothing to do with biology. It's about drawing pyramids to show what age groups you've got in different populations. So there.

Q1. Complete this description of population pyramids and structures:

A population pyramid is a diagram showing how a place's population is made up (its "structure"). It divides the people into .... groups and gives the % of .... and .... in each. If the pyramid has a wide base, that tells you that there are a lot of .... If the top quickly becomes very ...., that tells you that on average people don't live well into old age.

Q2. Here are two oddly shaped pyramids, A and B. Look at them and answer the questions.

a) Is the birth rate in A <u>quite high</u> or <u>quite low</u>?

....

b) In A, how many people live beyond the age of 70 — <u>a lot</u> or <u>a few</u>?

....

c) Describe the % of young men in A aged 20-40 — is it <u>high</u> or <u>low</u>?

....

d) Describe the % of elderly people in B — is it <u>high</u> or <u>low</u>?

....

e) In pyramid B, there are few people aged 20-40. They haven't died, so what is the likely reason for these small numbers of people?

....

f) Now you should be able to decide which pyramid is which: one is Eastbourne, a seaside resort on the south coast of England with a pleasant climate. The other is Bombay in India, a port and industrial area with jobs that attract a lot of workers from other parts of India.

Which is A? ....   Which is B? ....

Section One — Population

Population Structure

Q3. Look at these pyramid shapes and complete the following sentences, using the words "low", "high" or "falling". Then identify which pyramid shape best fits each stage in the model. You can look back to the diagram of the Demographic Transition Model (page 5) to help you.

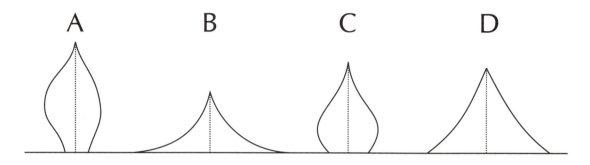

a) In Stage 1 the birth rate is .... and the death rate is .... = Pyramid ....

b) In Stage 2 the birth rate is .... and the death rate is falling = Pyramid ....

c) In Stage 3 the birth rate is falling, and the death rate is .... = Pyramid ....

d) In Stage 4 the birth rate is ...., and the death rate is .... = Pyramid ....

Q4. Define the term "infant mortality rate".

....

Q5. Which of these is the correct definition of "high life expectancy"? Tick the right answer.

a) People can expect to live for many years (e.g. up to 70 and over). ☐

b) People look forward to lots of parties and clubbing. ☐

Q6. What is meant by the "economically active population"?

....

So it's true — Eastbourne IS full of old dears...
What I want to know is... what I want to know is, right... what did you take Geography for? Was it all those volcanoes and earthquakes that persuaded you... thought so. You hadn't counted on all this had you. No, well... you're stuck with it now, so your only option is learn it pal.

Section One — Population

Population Structure and Dependency

Dependency: "how many children and old people there are scrounging off the middle-aged tax-payers" — well that's what my dad says...

Q1. What is the formula for working out the dependency ratio?

....

Q2. A group of aliens have set up a colony on Mars. 5000 aliens work in the factories there, making the red paint to paint the planet with. They have 2000 children and there are 500 elderly aliens who just sit around all day playing bingo. Work out the dependency ratio for this population.

....

....

Q3. Circle the correct word(s) in each pair below.

High numbers of young dependants occur in MEDCs/LEDCs, where the dependency ratio can be over 100/under 50. This means that a lot of money is needed for health care and education/exotic holidays. As these children grow up, they in turn will have few/lots of children, causing a population decline/explosion. All these people will then need food, jobs and houses/CD players. All these will be in short supply, so that the country will be under/over populated.

Q4. In the following list circle the four things needed in an MEDC when there are high numbers of elderly dependants.

Doctors and hospitals   Playgroups   Buses and trains   Discos

Skateboard parks   Sheltered housing   Nursing homes

Q5. Fill in the gaps to finish off these descriptions of long-term problems facing Britain with its large numbers of elderly dependants:

a) The birth rate is .... and so the population total may ....

b) The elderly have to be supported financially by the .... population.

c) As time passes, the % of elderly people .... , so that the problem never goes away.

Q6. Which of these is a typical Dependency Ratio for an MEDC and which is typical of an LEDC?

a) 50-70 is typical for an ....

b) over 100 is typical for an ....

You and I are gonna live forever...

It's pretty easy stuff. Learn that dependency ratio formula and the rest's just common sense.

Section One — Population

Managing Population Growth

"Managing population growth" = stopping your population getting too big. You have to learn this, because it's a real big issue for countries like China who've had to slam the brakes on big time.

Q1. Which of these has to be reduced to slow down population growth? Tick the correct box.

a) The birth rate. ☐

b) The death rate. ☐

Q2. Which of these is the most serious problem if a country has a population explosion:

a) Providing education. ☐

b) Providing food. ☐

Q3. State <u>two</u> ways in which LEDC governments can encourage a lower birth rate.

1. ....

2. ....

Q4. Give <u>two</u> reasons why it's difficult to have a birth control policy in some LEDCs.

1. ....

2. ....

Q5. Complete this diagram to show how poor diet and poor health worsen population problems:

unhealthy
....

unhealthy mothers

high i..........................
m..........................

poor diet, food shortage

too many children to feed

more children are born resulting in high .... rate

Q6. Circle the LEDC that has successfully managed to reduce birth rates and improve health:

Ethiopa   India

Bangladesh

Section One — Population

Managing Population Growth

Q7. Read this case study about China and then answer the questions:

> In 1949, most people in China lived in poverty and suffered poor health. The birth rate was high (45 per 1000) and life expectancy was only 32. Agriculture was disorganised and food production was low. Many died in famines. There was a lot of unemployment and little industry. In the 1970s the government encouraged people to reduce the birth rate and in 1979 the policy of one child per family started. Also people were not given permission to marry until they were 22. By 1994 the birth rate had fallen to 22 per 1000. Farming was much improved and industry was flourishing after the discovery of large reserves of coal.

   a) Was China over- or under-populated in 1949? ....

   b) State three facts that led to your answer to a)

   1. ....

   2. ....

   3. ....

   c) Give two reasons for the low life expectancy in 1949.

   1. ....

   2. ....

   d) Which two rules set up by the government successfully reduced the population growth?

   1. ....

   2. ....

   e) Had the birth rate fallen by approx. 33%, 25% or 50% by 1994? ....

Q8. Fill in the table which shows different ways to increase food supplies in the world to feed the growing population:

Scheme	Description	Examples	Problems Caused
I..................	Watering of dry areas for crops	MEDC .... LEDC	
Draining of marshes	Drains and pumping stations remove excess water from wetlands	MEDC	
F..................	Chemicals to improve the soil quality	MEDC .... LEDC — India in the Green Revolution	
P..................	Chemicals to kill off insect pests and weeds	MEDC	

Hey, you there — I said one child only...

It sounds a bit sad, only one child per family in China — that means no brothers or sisters. BUT for the exam you have to know why China (and other countries) have to watch their populations.

Section One — Population

Migration

Birds migrate, people migrate — but this is <u>human</u> geography, ignore the birds and answer these questions.

Q1. What do we call a person who moves from place to place?

    ....

Q2. Answers these questions about the <u>three</u> types of migration.

   a) Define "international migration".

    ....

   b) What type of migration would a move from rural Wales to London be called?

    ....

   c) What is the third type of migration?

    ....

Q3. Look at the diagram below and answer the questions.

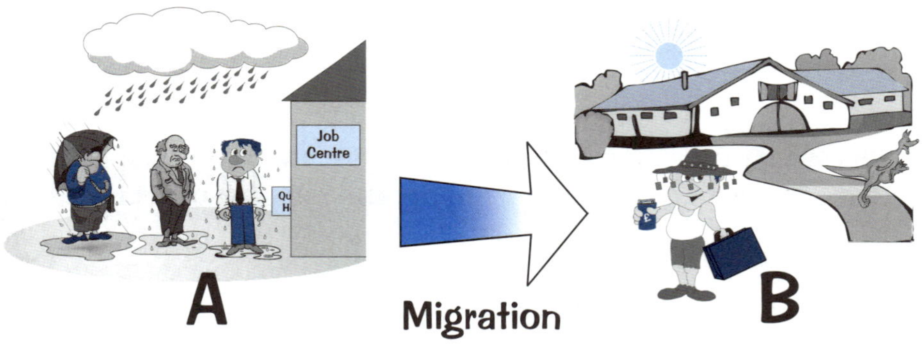

A → Migration → **B**

   a) State <u>two</u> reasons why people might want to leave area A.

    ....
    ....

   b) These reasons are called p.................... factors.

   c) State <u>two</u> reasons why people would be attracted to area B.

    ....
    ....

   d) These reasons are called the p.................... factors.

<u>Migration — it's a moving topic for sure...</u>
People have loads of different reasons to move from one place to another — to get a job, for a better standard of living, to escape war, for nicer weather, to escape the smog, for a laugh...

Section One — Population

Types of Migration

Gone are the days when no one went further than four miles out of the village. Nowadays people move about all over the place — for the exam, you need to know <u>why</u>.

Q1. Many people came to Britain from India in the 1950s. This is an example of international migration from an LEDC to an MEDC. Give <u>three</u> reasons why people made this move.

1. ....
2. ....
3. ....

Q2. Answer these questions about international migration from one MEDC to another MEDC.

a) Give one reason why many British people move to Spain.

....

b) Give one reason why many British people move to Canada.

....

c) What is meant by the 'brain drain'?

....

Q3. The list shows factors which cause regional migration (e.g. rural to urban moves in LEDCs). Write out the push and pull factors under the right headings.

farming is poor;   better education;   few jobs;
poor sanitation;   more hospitals;   place is busy and modern.

<u>A remote village in Mexico — PUSH</u>   <u>Mexico City — PULL</u>

....
....
....

Q4. Answer these questions on counterurbanisation in MEDCs (e.g. Britain).

a) What is "counterurbanisation"?

....

b) What is the name for the daily migration that has increased because of counterurbanisation?

....

c) Circle the type of transport that has increased counterurbanisation the most.

aeroplanes   trains   cars   rollerblades

Section One — Population

Types of Migration

Q5. Answer these questions about the migration of refugees.

a) Describe two push factors that cause refugees to move.

1. ....

2. ....

b) Name an example of a refugee movement.

....

Q6. Migration can be controlled by governments. Suggest what a government could do to encourage people to move out of crowded areas into quieter areas.

....

....

....

....

....

Q7. Name one example for each of the following <u>types</u> of migration.

a) International migration from an LEDC to an MEDC

....

b) International migration from an MEDC to an MEDC

....

c) Regional migration from a rural area to an urban area

....

d) Local migration in an MEDC

....

e) Forced migration (refugees)

....

I'm leaving on a jet plane — couldn't afford to get in it...

Because migration is all pretty much common sense, your mind can go blank when they ask for reasons. The trick is to remember a whole load of reasons why someone would migrate, then pick and choose which ones apply to the question you're being asked. I'd write some lists now.

Section One — Population

Section Two — Settlement

Houses and Stuff

This is all about why villages, towns and cities grew up where they did (eg near rivers and roads).

Q1. Give a brief definition of the term "settlement".
....

Q2. Define the "site" of a settlement.
....

Q3. What is meant by the "situation" of a settlement?
....

Q4. Explain what's meant by "site factors" and name one factor.
....

Q5. Use the diagram to answer these questions:

Settlement Sites

(Diagram showing settlements at positions A (on chalk hillside), B (on hilltop), C (by river), D (at river crossing), with Chalk and Clay layers; legend shows Road, River, Settlement)

a) Which site factor led to the choice of sites marked A? ....

b) Settlements like A are known as .... settlements.

c) Give two reasons for the choice of site B. ....
....

d) Give two reasons for the choice of site C. ....
....

e) Give one reason for the choice of site D.
....

f) Site D is known as a De............... Site.

g) Which other site (A, B or C) is also a good example of the name in f)? ....

h) Which settlement is the best example of a dry point site? ....

i) Describe two other important things that early settlers would need to have nearby.
....
....

Site and situation — new novel by Jane Austen...

This stuff is fairly easy as long as you stay awake. But you do have to stay awake. Get the matchsticks.

The Settlement Hierarchy

The bigger the settlement, the fewer of them there are. Oops, think I've given the game away...

Q1. Finish off the labels on this diagram to show the settlement hierarchy.

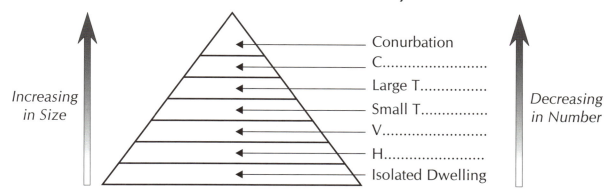

The Settlement Hierarchy

Increasing in Size → Conurbation / C............... / Large T............... / Small T............... / V............... / H............... / Isolated Dwelling ← Decreasing in Number

Q2. Look at this graph of settlements in Shropshire:

Scattergraph of population and number of services in Shropshire

a) Define "services" in relation to settlements.

....

....

b) What happens to the number of services as settlement size increases?

....

c) Does this graph show a positive or negative correlation? ....

d) In the following list circle the three which are often found in small villages:

post office;   jeweller's shop;   a corner shop;   an infant school;   a university.

e) Why do villages not have the other two in the above list?

....

f) Are the three that you circled in d) called low or high order services?

....

g) What is the name for the type of services found in larger settlements?

....

Settlement Hierarchy — what a bundle of laughs...

When you look over the page, it's not exactly rocket science. The problem with the easier stuff is you get caught out thinking you don't need to pay full attention. Don't waste those easy marks.

Section Two — Settlement

The Sphere of Influence of a Settlement

My mum used to drive for an hour to the next town just to go shopping.
That's exactly what this 'sphere of influence' stuff is about...

Q1. Look at the diagram of a town and its sphere of influence, then answer the questions.

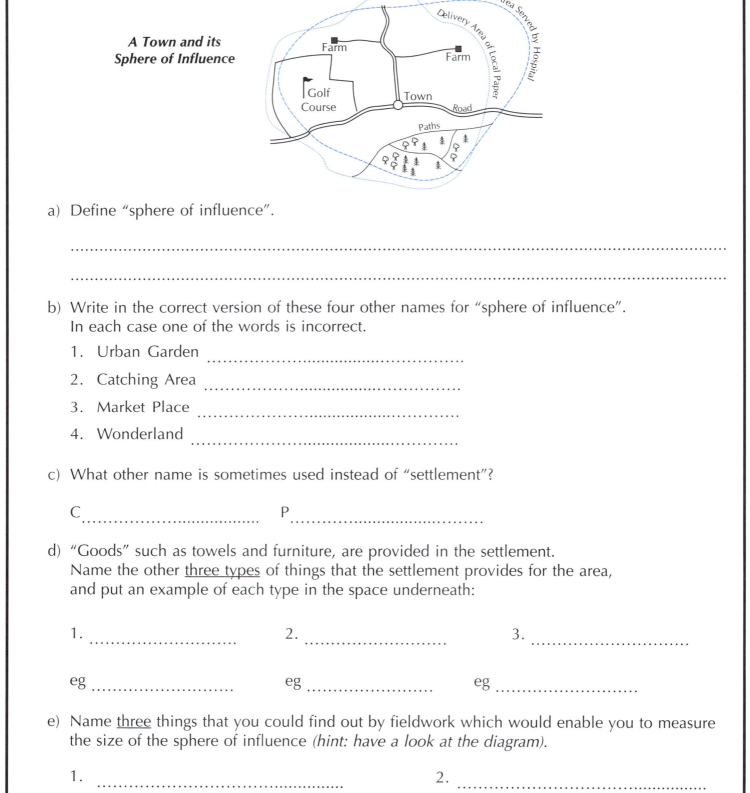

A Town and its Sphere of Influence

a) Define "sphere of influence".

  ....

  ....

b) Write in the correct version of these four other names for "sphere of influence". In each case one of the words is incorrect.

  1. Urban Garden   ....
  2. Catching Area ....
  3. Market Place   ....
  4. Wonderland   ....

c) What other name is sometimes used instead of "settlement"?

  C............................   P............................

d) "Goods" such as towels and furniture, are provided in the settlement.
   Name the other <u>three types</u> of things that the settlement provides for the area, and put an example of each type in the space underneath:

  1. ....   2. ....   3. ....

  eg ....   eg ....   eg ....

e) Name <u>three</u> things that you could find out by fieldwork which would enable you to measure the size of the sphere of influence *(hint: have a look at the diagram)*.

  1. ....   2. ....

  3. ....

Section Two — Settlement

The Sphere of Influence of a Settlement

Q2. Does a village have a large or small sphere of influence? Explain your answer.

....

....

Q3. Does a city have a large or small sphere of influence? Explain your answer.

....

....

Q4. Look at the diagram. Then correct the paragraph below, by circling the correct words in the eight pairs:

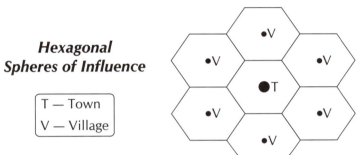

Hexagonal Spheres of Influence

T — Town
V — Village

Town T serves its own small local area, and the areas of the surrounding villages V

In an ideal world, people in the villages "V" would obtain low/high order goods like cameras/milk from their own village. They would travel a short/long distance for these. They would travel further to town "T" for middle order goods like a bank/some stamps. This makes T's sphere of influence smaller/larger than V's and it is made up of seven/four small spheres of influence. When people want the theatre or other low/high order goods and services they will travel further still — to the city, which therefore has an even larger/smaller sphere of influence.

Q5. Who put forward this theory of hexagons, based on settlements in Germany?

....

a) Why did he use hexagons instead of circles?

....

b) What is this theory called?

....

Spear of influence — when Geography turns bad...

When they ask about the spheres of influence of cities and villages, try thinking of places you <u>know</u>. Turn them into Manchester and Little Mackerel (or wherever) in your head and think what they're like.

Section Two — Settlement

Urban Land Use in MEDC Cities

"Urban land use" — words to strike drowsiness into the heart of even the most hardened Geographer.

Q1. Answer the questions about this model of urban land use.

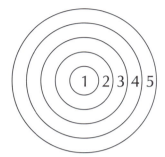

a) Complete the labels of the land use zones.

1. ....
2. ....
3. ....
4. ....
5. ....

b) Who created this model?

....

c) According to this model, which zone contains the original site of the city?

....

d) According to this model, where are the newest developments?

....

Q2. Look at this diagram of another model of land use in a city and answer the questions.

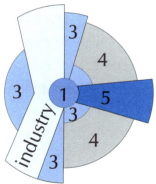

a) What is this model called?

....

b) Who created it?

....

c) Why are some zones in lines or wedges?

....

d) Which zone is exactly the same in both models?

....

Section Two — Settlement

Urban Land Use in MEDC Cities

Q3. Correct this paragraph about the Central Business District by circling the correct words in the ten pairs.

The Characteristics of the CBD

The CBD is at the edge/**heart** of the city. It is the busy **shopping**/manufacturing centre, and every day thousands of people come in to work in the airport/**offices**. Many roads and rail routes lead to the CBD. There is a low/**high** density of buildings, and many are **multi-storey**/bungalows, because there is a lot of/**shortage of** space. The competition for space forces land values **up**/down, and this means that mostly **famous-name**/small individual stores are found here. **High**/low land values also means that the residential population is very **low**/high.

Q4. What is the "urban fringe"? (Tick the correct answer)

a) ☐ A new and fantastically trendy hairstyle.

b) ☐ The edge of a city.

There's no easy way to say this Mrs Johnstone... ...your husband has been demolished as part of the CBD improvement scheme.

Q5. What is a "greenfield site"?

....

....

Q6. Some people live in villages on the city edge but commute to the city to work. What are these villages called?

....

My, what a high class residential urban fringe you have, Mr Burgess...

Ah... Mr Hoyt and Mr Burgess — where'd we be without them. Get those two city models firmly in your head, then the rest'll sink in much more easily. There's a load of jargon in this bit as well, which is a pain, but it'll really impress the markers if you can come out with it in your exam.

Section Two — Settlement

Urbanisation

I know why people move to the city — more places to have exams in. Maybe.

Q1. Define "urbanisation".

....

Q2. The table below shows the populations of some of the world's largest cities:

CITY	1985	2000	
Mexico City	17.3	25.8	
London	10.4	10.5	*(all figures in millions)*
Sao Paulo	15.9	24.0	
New York	15.6	15.8	

a) Describe the rate of growth in LEDC cities compared to MEDC cities.

....

....

b) Give <u>two</u> reasons for what is happening to the growth rate of the LEDC cities.

1. ....

2. ....

Q3. Urbanisation in LEDCs has many negative effects on the rural areas.
Complete this list of effects, choosing answers from the phrases below.

> - the young have left and there are fewer and fewer children.
> - the elderly population is less able to do difficult, physical work.
> - those of working age have left.
> - elderly.
> - invests little money in rural areas.
>
> *(use each once only)*

a) It is mainly young adults who go to the cities, and so the population becomes...

....

b) Farming in rural areas declines because...

....

c) Poverty continues in rural areas because the Government...

....

d) Family life and customs break down because...

....

e) Growth of employment and wealth does not occur in rural areas because...

....

Herbanisation — thyme to move to the city...

Cities are *great*. *Everyone* should live in a city. There are loads of *services* and *lovely people*.

Section Two — Settlement

Counterurbanisation

Counterurbanisation. Tongue twister, score of 23 in scrabble... and an important geography topic.

Q1. Define "counterurbanisation". Does it occur in the LEDCs or MEDCs?

....
....
....
....

Q2. Look at this picture and give <u>four</u> push factors it illustrates that help to cause counterurbanisation:

1. ....
   ....
2. ....
   ....
3. ....
   ....
4. ....
   ....

Q3. Give one example of how Government policy can encourage counterurbanisation.

....
....

Q4. State <u>two</u> other reasons for counterurbanisation.

1. ....
   ....
2. ....
   ....

Counterherbanisation — thyme to move back...
Cities are *rubbish*. *No one* should live in a city. There are loads of *traffic jams* and *muggers*.

Section Two — Settlement

Problems in MEDC Cities

In theory, the centre of a town is where all the best bits are. In a lot of places, that ain't the case...

Q1. Answer these questions:
   a) Why have many factories in the inner city been abandoned? (Give two reasons.)
      1. ....
      ....
      2. ....
      ....

   b) Give one reason why it is difficult to attract new businesses into the inner city.
      ....
      ....

   c) What has happened to employment in the inner city?
      ....
      ....

   d) What state are the original houses in and why?
      ....
      ....

   e) Many inner city areas are "deprived areas". What does "deprived" mean?
      ....

   f) Inner city areas often have a shortage of "social amenities". What does this mean?
      ....
      ....

Q2. Give two ways in which air pollution from traffic can be reduced in cities.
      1. ....
      ....
      2. ....
      ....

Q3. Correct this paragraph, by circling the right words in the pairs:

   The Army/The Government has stepped in since 1945 to help the inner city. Schemes called removal schemes/urban renewal schemes have been set up (e.g. in London and Birmingham). They aim to do three things:
   1) Replace old houses with clubs and theatres/new housing.
   2) Create jobs in light industry/heavy industry like steel.
   3) Build more shops, clinics, sports facilities/power stations and multi storey car parks.

Section Two — Settlement

Problems in MEDC Cities

Q4. Look at the diagram and answer the questions which follow.

a) State <u>two</u> push factors which are causing shops and offices to move out of the CBD.

   1. ....
   2. ....

b) State <u>two</u> reasons why they are "pulled" to out of town locations in retail or business parks.

   1. ....
   2. ....

c) Name an example of one of these out of town sites, and name the city it is near.

   ....

d) Some shops move out of the old CBD into new shopping malls.
   Give <u>two</u> reasons why the shopping malls attract them.

   1. ....
   2. ....

e) Name an example of a shopping mall, saying which city it is in.

   ....

Q5. As factories and businesses abandon the city centre it becomes empty.
What name is given to this effect and in which country did it start?

   ....

We've gotta get out of this place — to an out of town development...
If you live in a town, you probably know some examples of businesses moving out of the CBD. Even ten years ago, most supermarkets and cinemas were in town centres. Go ask someone old.

Section Two — Settlement

Urban Problems of LEDCs

As you'd expect, the problems in LEDC cities are different from the problems in MEDC cities. Have no fear — here's two pages of questions so you can check if you're up to scratch.

Q1. Look at the simplified map of Mexico City.

- Rich Residential Areas
- Poor Housing and Shanties
- Industrial Areas
- Medium Quality
- City Centre
- City Edge
- Major Road

a) Are the poorest housing areas located near the centre or near the edge of the city?

....

b) Some of the people in the poor areas live over 20 km from their jobs. Describe two problems that they face as a result of this:

1. ....

2. ....

c) In which two types of location would you expect expensive housing to be found?

1. ....
2. ....

d) Describe the locations of the industrial areas (East? South? near..?)

....

e) Suggest two urban problems which are caused by the industrial areas.

1. ....
2. ....

f) Suggest two environmental problems which exist on the urban fringe, where people tend to build shanty towns.

1. ....
2. ....

Section Two — Settlement

Urban Problems of LEDCs

Q2. Correct this paragraph by circling the correct words in the pairs. Then complete the sentences below.

Sao Paulo, in Brazil, is one of the most rapidly/slowly growing cities in the world. Hundreds of migrants per day come from urban/rural areas. They set up shanties in the middle/on the edge of the city because there is a shortage/plenty of space in the city. The population is now over 24 million and many people live in crowded, poor conditions. This causes four basic problems for the city:

1) Providing clean w..........................
2) Providing w.......................... disposal for industries.
3) Providing a weekly r.......................... collection.
4) Providing a s.......................... system.

Q3. Tick true or false for each of these statements about LEDC cities:

T F
a) ☐ ☐ LEDC cities cannot provide enough health care for all.
b) ☐ ☐ Industrial air pollution causes a lot of ill health in LEDC cities.
c) ☐ ☐ Sewerage systems are coping with the city waste.
d) ☐ ☐ Water supplies and crops are often contaminated with sewage.
e) ☐ ☐ Shanty towns are often built on dangerous rubbish tips.
f) ☐ ☐ Travelling across LEDC cities is easy and quick.

Q4. Draw four lines to match up the halves of these mixed up sentences.

A Migrants arrive in the city in such great numbers

B People are encouraged to improve their shanties

C The Government wants to help the poor

D Many LEDCs owe huge debts to MEDCs, leaving them unable to cope with the urban poor

1 but money is short.

2 and so city problems continue to grow.

3 that it's impossible to give an accurate figure for the city population.

4 by self-help schemes, eg the city authorities provide bricks and cement for them.

Geography, geography, geography — my three favourite words...
This stuff isn't much fun, but you've got to learn it for the exam. I saw Davina McCall on Comic Relief visiting a shanty town in Africa, where the people lived in terrible conditions. Makes you think.

Section Two — Settlement

Planning and the Rural-Urban Fringe

The last page on towns and planning... Take a deep breath, and go for your life on them answers.

Q1. Give a definition of:

a) The "rural-urban fringe".

....
....

b) The "urban sprawl".

....
....

Q2. Give <u>two</u> reasons why planners want to stop urban sprawl.

1. ....
....

2. ....
....

Q3. Name the type of migration in MEDCs that was causing urban sprawl.

....

Q4. Define "conurbation" and name an example.

....
....

Q5. Describe <u>three</u> types of leisure activity that go on in the rural-urban fringe.

1. ....
....

2. ....
....

3. ....
....

Rural-urban fringe — not a dodgy geographer's haircut...
If only everyone would stay put, none of this would be a problem. Sigh.

Section Three — Farming

Farming

There's more to farming than flat caps and chewing on dry grass. It's a vital industry producing food to match the needs of growing, developing populations, so you need to know about it...

Q1. Define "agriculture". ....

....

Q2. Why is it important to all countries? ....

....

Q3. Is it classed as a primary, secondary, tertiary or quaternary industry? ....

Q4. Read the paragraph about farming in East Anglia and then answer the questions:

> Mr Simpson's farm is small, with 210 hectares of land. He grows wheat, barley, beans and sugar beet. The land is well suited to these being flat, fairly dry and not too high (altitude 30 m above sea level). The climate in this rain shadow part of Britain is drier than most areas and the average rainfall is 590 mm per year which is fine for these crops. Summers are warm and dry for harvesting. The soil is chalky and alkaline, which the farmer improves with the addition of organic matter (dead leaves of beet and the straw and stalks of the other crops). He also adds chemical fertilisers. The farm is run by two full-time and two part-time workers and much of the work is done by machinery. There are special buildings to house the tractors and other machines. The farmer's products are beans for animal feed, sugar beet (which is processed for sugar leaving the pulp to be made into animal feed), wheat (for flour) and barley (for beer making).

a) Describe the physical inputs to this farming system.

   1. Climate ....

   ....

   2. Soils ....

   ....

   3. Relief ....

   ....

b) Describe the economic inputs (anything to do with money).

   ....

   ....

c) List the outputs ....

d) Name the two things which make up the feedback to this system.
   1. .... 2. ....

e) The farmer is important in the system because he is a "decision maker".
   Suggest three things that he has to make decisions about on this farm.
   1. ....
   2. ....
   3. ....

Near ming or far ming? — I'll get my coat...

Don't take your farmers for granted, a'ight.

Classifying Farming

Farming comes in all different flavours - except we don't call them flavours, we call them classifications. It might be a longer word but have you tried licking a farm?

Q1. Define the three types of farms below by choosing the correct definitions.
This is an example of classification by type of farm produce.

They specialise in animal rearing.

They specialise in growing crops.

They have both animals and crops.

Arable farms:

....

Pastoral farms:

....

Mixed farms:

....

Q2. Circle the correct words in each pair below.

a) <u>Intensive Farms</u>.

Intensive farms produce a high/low yield per hectare and inputs are low/high. The inputs can be money and technology, eg: on a Welsh hill sheep farm/in a market garden in Worcestershire where farmers need to buy a lot of fertiliser and special equipment. Also intensive farms can have a low/high input of labour, which is common in MEDCs/LEDCs, such as rice farming in Bangladesh.

b) <u>Extensive farming</u>.

Extensive farms tend to be large/small and are often on land which is good/poor. These farms have many/few workers but because of the size of these farms, yields can still be high. An example of an extensive farm is a wheat farm in the Canadian Prairies/ East Anglia.

Q3. Define the following words.

a) "pesticide"

....

b) "fertiliser"

....

Classifying Farming

Q4. Answer these questions about classification of a farm by its purpose.

a) Some farmers produce things to feed themselves. Name this type of farming.

....

b) Other farms produce things for sale. Name this type of farming.

....

c) An example of type a) is "shifting cultivation". Explain what is meant by shifting cultivation.

....

....

d) Name an area of the world that has shifting cultivation. ....

e) What is the name for crops that are grown to be sold? ....

f) Define "factory farming" and give an example.

....

....

Q5. Now classify these examples of farming. Each one needs three words, one from each of the ideas in Q1, 2 and 4. The first one is done for you.

a) A dairy farm of 140 hectares, Somerset. *A pastoral, intensive, commercial farm.*

b) A tea plantation in India. ....

c) A large sheep station (farm) in the Australian Outback. ....

d) A farm producing bulbs and flowers in Holland. ....

e) Vine growing in California. ....

f) A peasant's two hectare plot of vegetables in Nepal. ....

g) A British battery chicken farm. ....

Show me your onions...
To classify a farm 'all' you need to ask is (...wait for it...) 'is the produce animals, crops or both', 'is the input intensive or extensive', 'is the purpose subsistence or commercial'...
That's 'all' you see — easy.

Section Three — Farming

Distribution of Farming Types

Different types of farms are found in different places.
"What farms?", "where?" and "why?" I hear you cry — calm your passions, it's all in here...

Q1. Look at the map and describe the <u>distribution</u> of arable farming and sheep farming.

Hint – remember that the "distribution" of things is all about describing WHERE they are.

You need to refer to North, South, West and East of England. Then get an atlas to help you and say whether the areas are <u>lowland</u> or <u>highland</u> and name the areas too.

a) arable farming
....
....

b) sheep farming
....
....

Q2. What are the three physical factors that affect farming types?

1. ....
2. ....
3. ....

Q3. Complete this paragraph about "Farming in Temperate Latitudes".

In the Temperate Latitudes (where it is neither too h......... nor too c............), farms are mostly c........................ farms. They can be a............... farms, eg growing maize in France; p..................... farms, eg sheep farms in New Zealand; or m..................... farms, eg wheat and cattle in the Midlands. There are i............ve farms such as the organic farms in Britain, and e..................ve farms such as sheep farming in Australia.

The Temperate Latitudes are mostly .... EDCs.

<u>What's hot and steamy and comes out of Cowes — the Isle of Wight ferry...</u>

That was about as exciting as a sheep farming holiday in the Hebrides — but if you don't know the different types of farms and where they are you're going to lose marks in the exam. Momma told me there'd be days like this.

Section Three — Farming

Farming in the EU — Economics and Politics

Farming in the EU has pros and cons. It has modern technology but is restricted by lots of rules — the rules themselves have lots of pros and cons — confused yet? You will be...

Q1. The EU introduced the CAP for all its countries, eg Britain. What does CAP stands for?

C.............................. A.............................. P..............................

Q2. How did the CAP protect European farmers from outside competition?

....

....

Q3. What were the original aims of the CAP?

1. to increase .... 2. to improve farm ....

Q4. By the 1980s the CAP had resulted in two very serious problems which are shown in the diagrams. Write notes in the boxes on the diagrams to explain what had happened.

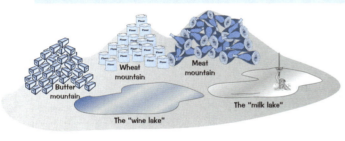 

....	....
....	....
....	....
....	....

Q5. The EU set up four schemes to deal with these problems. Complete these statements about the schemes.

a) The Q.............. system to reduce the over-production of ....

b) The S.............. A.............. Schemes to reduce the over-production of ....

c) D.............. Schemes to reduce farm production and to allow farmers to earn money from other activities on their farms such as ....

d) The protection of the en.............................. in certain areas which were called

E.............. S.............. Areas.

Section Three — Farming

Farming in the EU — Economics and Politics

Q6. Answer these questions about the CAP and milk production.

a) What did the Government do after World War II to encourage farmers to produce more milk?
....

b) But by the 1980s too much was being produced, and so what did the EU do?
....

c) Fill in the speech bubbles in the diagram. The man from the Government is explaining about quotas and the farmer is explaining how quotas make things very difficult for him.

....
....
....
....

Q7. Complete this explanation of set aside schemes:

"All farms over 20 hectares must take .... % of their land out of production for at least .... years. Farmers are paid a s................... to compensate them for loss of earnings."

Q8. Answer these questions about diversification schemes.

a) Define "diversification schemes". ....
....

b) Name four different types of diversification activities that occur on farms.

1. .... 3. ....
2. .... 4. ....

Q9. The Government realised over-farming the landscape of Britain was causing damage so they set up Environmentally Sensitive Areas (ESAs) in certain areas to try and protect the environment.

a) Look at the map, and name the ESAs shown.

1. The Yorkshire D..........................
2. The .... District.
3. The .... Broads.
4. The South ....

b) Explain how farmers are encouraged to help in these areas.
....
....

What's tangy and tells you how to farm — the European Onion...
See what I mean. Pros and cons, pros and cons...

Section Three — Farming

Modern Farming in MEDCs

In MEDCs farming has become a modern business.
If you still think of farming equipment as an old stick and an ox — things have changed...

Q1. Look at these two sketches and then answer the questions:

Britain 1945   Britain 2001

a) Describe eight differences between these two pictures. The first one is done for you:

1. 1945 – machines simpler and pulled by horses. 2001 – machines bigger, with engines and needing fuel.
2. ....
3. ....
4. ....
5. ....
6. ....
7. ....
8. ....

b) Explain two environmental problems which are caused by modern farming techniques like those in the picture.

1. ....
2. ....

Q2. Since 1945, miles of hedgerows have been removed in Britain in order to make farming more efficient. Fill in these points to show why hedgerows are removed and why this causes problems:

Reasons for removing hedgerows	Why hedgerows are important in the environment.
1.	1. ....
2.	2. ....
3.	3. ....

More tractors — more machines — a-ha-ha-ha...
The bigger the machines, the bigger the fields. Removing hedgerows is all about money, and keeping them is all about the environment. It's a classic conflict of interest. Tricky.

Section Three — Farming

Farming in LEDCs

The age old geography question — the difference between LEDCs and MEDCs. So if the previous page was farming in MEDCs, this page could only be LEDCs — not such a mystery this question lark is it.

Q1. Many farmers in LEDCs are very poor (eg: in Nepal and Bangladesh). Read this account of farming in Nepal and then answer the questions:

> Nepal, in the Himalayas, has a very rapidly growing population and it is becoming increasingly difficult to provide enough food. It is difficult to find suitable land on the steep slopes and so the land is terraced but plots are very small (often under two hectares). The people work hard to try and grow food for themselves and to find grazing land for their animals but the soil becomes exhausted. Trees have been removed and animals graze on everything. In the heavy monsoon rains, the loose soil is washed away and there are landslides, destroying the terraces.

   a) What kind of farming is described here — commercial or subsistence? ....

   b) Are the outputs high or low? ....

   c) Is this intensive or extensive farming? ....

   d) Describe one <u>human</u> factor which is causing problems in food supply.
   ....

   e) Describe one <u>physical</u> factor which is causing problems in food supply.
   ....

   f) Name two environmental problems that are caused by farmers in Nepal.
   1. ....   2. ....

   g) Explain why these farmers in Nepal cannot improve their farming output.
   ....

Q2. Name <u>two</u> other examples of this type of farming in LEDCs, saying which country they are in.

   1. ....   2. ....

Q3. Answer these questions about plantations.

   a) Some farms in LEDCs, such as plantations, are very wealthy businesses. Define "plantation".
   ....

   b) Are plantations commercial or subsistence farms? ....

   c) Give two examples of plantation farming, saying which LEDC they are in and naming the crop in each case.

   1. ....   2. ....

   d) Plantations are often examples of monoculture. Define "monoculture".
   ....

Section Three — Farming

Farming in LEDCs

Q4. Read this account of farming in Kenya and then answer the questions.

> Like Nepal, Kenya has problems providing food for its rapidly growing population. The people who need to grow subsistence crops and keep a few animals have been forced off their land by large multinational companies who now own the best farmland. These foreign-owned companies own huge areas of plantations, producing cash crops for export such as tea and coffee. These companies are wealthy but the local farmers become poorer because their attempts to farm the poorest, least productive land causes soil erosion by rain in the wet season, and by the wind in the dry season.

a) Name two cash crops that are produced in Kenya.

   1. .... 2. ....

b) Who owns the plantations? ....

c) Where does most of the profit of the plantations go? ....

d) What effect has the plantation system had on local farmers?
   ....

e) What environmental problem has resulted? ....

f) What's the name for land which is really unsuitable for farming (eg: it is too dry, or too stony).
   It's called M.............................. Land.

Q5. Answer these questions about plantations. (Yes, more of them. You love it.)

a) Name a case study of plantation farming that you have studied. ....
b) Fill in the advantages and disadvantages of plantation farming.

The advantages of plantations:	The disadvantages of plantations:
1.	1. ....
2.	2. ....
3.	3. ....

Cash crop — so money does grow on trees...

The same comparisons between MEDCs and LEDCs pop up left, right and centre. Both have problems, but they are very different. You must understand what these differences are, why they occur and how the different countries cope with their problems.

Section Three — Farming

The Green Revolution

The 'Green Revolution' sounds like it should involve a load of people called Boggy and Snowdrip tying themselves to trees — but it's actually about major changes in farming technology...

Q1. Tick True or False for these statements about the Green Revolution.

    T F

a) ☐ ☐ The Green Revolution is the name for changes in farming in MEDCs.

b) ☐ ☐ The Green Revolution is the name for changes in farming in LEDCs.

c) ☐ ☐ It began in the 1960s.

d) ☐ ☐ It began in the 1900s.

e) ☐ ☐ It was introduced because of the need to increase the output of cash crops.

f) ☐ ☐ It was introduced because of the need to increase outputs of subsistence crops.

g) ☐ ☐ The Green Revolution is an example of intensive, subsistence farming.

Q2. Finish off these two sentences, to show why the Green Revolution was needed.

a) Food supply was a problem because of rapid p............ g............ .

b) Food supply was a problem because of very low y............ on the farms.

Q3. What are HYVs and what did they do to crop outputs?

....

Q4. Answer these questions.
a) Which two crops helped to increase food production in Mexico?

1. .... 2. ....

b) Which crop helped to increase food production in the Philippines? ....

c) Name two other areas where the Green Revolution occurred.

1. .... 2. ....

Q5. Explain the four ways in which HYVs increase farmers' yields.

1. ....

2. ....

3. ....

4. ....

Section Three — Farming

The Green Revolution

Q6. Circle the correct description of the Green Revolution – only one of these is correct:

Alternative energy.   Appropriate technology.   Hi-tech industry.

Q7. The exam might get you to write a short essay about the successes and failures of the Green Revolution (meaning its advantages and disadvantages). Sort out these sentences and then copy them into the lists below.

Rice production has doubled.

Some farms are very small and farmers can't afford the new seeds and fertiliser.

New farming methods have created new jobs eg: drivers, mechanics.

People have surplus food to sell and therefore have more money.

There are new jobs in factories making farm chemicals.

The use of machinery has caused farm workers to lose their jobs.

Many farm workers migrate to the cities, adding to the urban problems.

Two crops per year are possible with irrigation. People are healthier.

Poorer farmers are afraid to change to new methods.

Schemes for borrowing money are not well developed.

The successes and failures of the Green Revolution in Malaysia.

Successes	Failures
....	....
....	....
....	....
....	....
....	....
....	....
....	....

A rolling toad — a green revolution...

The green revolution sounds like it should be all good news — developing technology and increasing food production. But nothing's ever all good news. Development can bring a load of new environmental and economic problems — so make sure you understand both sides of the coin.

Farming and the Environment

Youngsters these days are pumped full of information about protecting the environment. But that's only 'cos it's really important. Now you have a chance to save the world and get good exam marks as well.

Q1. Answer these questions about desertification.

   a) Define "desertification". ....
   ....

   b) Look at the map and fill in the spaces in the key to name the areas shown.

   1. The South West of ...., including the states of C..................., A................... and N................... M...................

   2. The North East of B...................

   3. The interior of Ar................... in South America.

   4. Lands to the North of the S................... desert eg: Al...................

   5. Large areas to the South of the S................... desert eg: E................... and S...................

   6. Areas of South A................... such as N...................

   7. Parts of the M................... E...................

   8. Areas of Asia such as P...................

   9. Southern I...................

   10. A lot of interior A...................

Q2. Finish off these explanations of the causes of desertification.

   a) Rapid population growth (eg: in Ethiopia) leads to def................... as people's demands for fuel increase.

   b) Overg................... in areas that are dry causes s................... e................... .

   c) Lands near deserts have unreliable rainfall patterns. In wetter years, farmers' herds increase but then in drought years, ...

   d) Plantation agriculture forces farmers onto marginal land, and their attempts to farm causes ....

Section Three — Farming

Farming and the Environment

Q3. Circle the two correct statements here:

Desertification is a problem in both MEDCs and LEDCs.   *It is very difficult to reverse the effects of desertification.*   *Desertification is easily reversed.*

Q4. Answer these questions about soil erosion:

a) Define "soil erosion". ....

b) Does it occur in LEDCS only, MEDCs only, or in both? ....

Q5. Name the two agents of erosion which are involved in soil erosion.

1. ....   2. ....

Q6. Look at the sketch and then explain carefully how ① to ⑥ cause soil erosion.

① Ploughing up & down steep slopes
② Deforestation of slopes
③ Overgrazing
④ Very large arable fields
⑤ Removal of hedgerows
⑥ Monoculture & chemicals

1. ....
2. ....
3. ....
4. ....
5. ....
6. ....

Q7. Name an example of each of the following (use a different example each time).

a) An LEDC where soil erosion by the rain has been caused by farming steep slopes. ....

b) An MEDC where soil erosion by wind occurs because the area is flat, dry and crop fields are very large. ....

c) An LEDC where overgrazing has caused soil erosion. ....

d) An MEDC where intensive arable farming and hedgerow removal has caused wind erosion. ....

Oo-ar — get orff my laand...

...So to sum up, the soil's been there for thousands of years and we come along and muck it all up. Tut. Anyway, to save the world (sorry, 'pass the exam') you need be able to scribble down what causes desertification and soil erosion. Most things, eg: deforestation, cause both.

Section Three — Farming

Section Four — Industry

The Classification of Industry

Hold on to your hats — it's the industry section. Whoop-de-doo...

Q1. Answer the following questions about primary industry.

a) What is primary industry?

    ....

b) (i) Circle the three industries in this list which are examples of a primary industry.

    bakery   coal mining   farming   car assembly   forestry

(ii) Which is the other primary industry, beginning with F? ....

c) What is the name given to the things produced by primary industries?

    r........................   m............................

Q2. Answer these questions about secondary industries.

a) What is a "secondary industry"?

    ....

b) Give two examples of a secondary industry.

    1. ....   2. ....

Q3. Answer these questions about tertiary industries.

a) What is a "tertiary industry"?

    ....

b) Give three examples of a tertiary industry.

    1. ....   2. ....   3. ....

Q4. Answer these questions about quaternary industries.

a) What is a "quaternary industry"?

    ....

b) Give two examples of a quaternary industry.

    1. ....   2. ....

The Classification of Industry

Q5. These figures show the % of the workforce employed in different types of industry in two different countries.

	Primary	Secondary	Tertiary / Quaternary
Country A	2	32	66
Country B	94	3	3

a) Which of these countries, A or B, is Nepal (LEDC)? ....

b) Which of these countries, A or B, is the USA (MEDC)? ....

c) Use one of the following words to complete each of the sentences.

    primary   secondary   tertiary   quaternary

In MEDCs most of the workforce is employed in .... industry.

In LEDCs most of the workforce is employed in .... industry.

Q6. Write these words in the <u>correct</u> boxes to show a bakery as a system.

    baking   cakes   labour force   flour

    money (capital)   sugar   bread   kneading dough

Inputs	Processes	Outputs

⬆ Feedback

Q7. Answer these questions about linkages in industry.

a) What is meant by "linkages" in industry?

....

b) Why is the car industry called "car assembly" rather than "car manufacturing"?

....

c) Name an advantage of linkages to the car industry.

....

d) Name a disadvantage of linkages to the car industry.

....

Do these questions 'industriously' — ah it's a cracker...

An easy start — a few questions about the different types of industry. The number of people working in each type of industry changes from country to country, and gives you a clue about the type of country it is. It's facts like this that make geography interesting, don't you know.

Section Four — Industry

The Location of Industry

Where you set up your business is vitally important — get it wrong and you're stuffed. It's got to be near your workers, near some roads or summat and sometimes near your market. Read on...

Q1. Draw a <u>line</u> between each labour force and the most suitable industry.

a) A large pool of unskilled workers.

b) A small number of highly qualified and highly trained staff.

c) A large skilled workforce.

1. A car assembly plant.

2. A research firm working on the latest computer technology.

3. A food packaging firm.

Q2. Transport costs are another factor in the location of industry.
Tick T (for True), or F (for False) for each of these statements:

T   F

a) ☐ ☐ In the 19th century, light products like jewellery were transported by rail.

b) ☐ ☐ In the 19th century, heavy bulky goods like coal were transported by rail.

c) ☐ ☐ Today, a location near a main road is more important than one near a railway.

d) ☐ ☐ Specialist goods like fresh flowers and unusual vegetables are often transported by air but this makes the selling price high.

e) ☐ ☐ If the raw materials are bulky and heavy but the finished product is lighter, then the best location for the factory is at the market.

f) ☐ ☐ If the finished product is big and bulky compared to the raw materials, then the best location for the factory is at the market.

Q3. Complete this table to give <u>two</u> advantages and <u>two</u> disadvantages of each form of transport used by industries.

	Road	Rail	Ship	Air
Advantages	1. 2.	1. 2.	1. 2.	1. 2.
Disadvantages	1. 2.	1. 2.	1. 2.	1. 2.

Section Four — Industry

The Location of Industry

Q4. Define the word "market" in relation to industry.

....

Q5. Name two different industries which usually locate near to the market, giving a different reason for each.

1. ....

Reason ....

2. ....

Reason ....

Q6. Answer the following questions about industrial agglomeration.

a) Define "industrial agglomeration".

....

b) Suggest two advantages of industrial agglomeration.

1. ....

2. ....

c) Look at the map and name the regions of industrial agglomeration shown.

1. ....

2. ....

3. ....

4. ....

5. ....

6. ....

Section Four — Industry

The Location of Industry

Q7. Two other factors concerning location of industry are the need for <u>suitable land</u> and <u>space</u>. Look at the diagram of the location of industry in a typical British city.

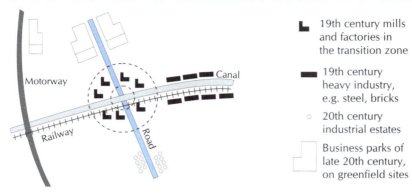

- 19th century mills and factories in the transition zone
- 19th century heavy industry, e.g. steel, bricks
- 20th century industrial estates
- Business parks of late 20th century, on greenfield sites

a) Describe <u>three</u> factors which led to the growth of factories in the transition zone.

1. .... 2. .... 3. ....

b) Where is the heavy industry located? Why is this?

....

....

c) Describe the location of the 20th century industry.
Why is it located here and not in the central business district or transition zone?

....

....

d) Describe the location of the business parks.
Give <u>three</u> reasons why they are in this type of location.

Location: ....

1. ....

2. ....

3. ....

e) Suggest three reasons why in recent years planners have encouraged industry back into the transition zone (inner city).

1. ....

2. ....

3. ....

Location, location, location...

Well I'll be jiggered — three pages (count 'em) on location of industries. You know what this means, don't you. That's right — it's an important topic and you have to know everything about it.

Section Four — Industry

Industry in LEDCs

If you like jargon, you'll love these pages. The last stuff was about the MEDCs and now it's time for the LEDCs. Great.

Q1. What is meant by the "formal sector" in LEDCs?

....

Q2. Answer these questions about the "informal sector".

a) What is the "informal sector"?

....

b) Give one reason why the informal sector is so important to many LEDCs.

....

c) Why can it be a disadvantage to work in the informal sector? Give one reason.

....

Q3. List each of the following industries under the correct column — formal or informal.

olive oil manufacturing   sewing and shoe repairs   pottery making
selling home-made snacks   children offering to be tourist guides   car washing
soft drinks manufacturing   leather tanning and making of bags

Formal	Informal
1.	1.
2.	2.
3.	3.
4.	4.

Q4 What are hours and wages like in the formal sector in LEDCs, compared to MEDCs?

....

Q5 Give two reasons why LEDCs find it difficult to develop industry by themselves.

1. ....

2. ....

"LEDC" — Learn Every Darn er... Cwestion...

Industries in LEDCs (Less Economically Developed Countries — don't forget) are different to those in MEDCs (More Economically Developed Countries). Large multinational companies often take advantage of the benefits of both types of country. Make sure you know how, or you'll regret it.

Section Four — Industry

The NICs

*Just when you thought the jargon was over — here come the NICs.
These are different from LEDCs — and examiners just love to test you to see if you know that.*

Q1. What does "NIC" stand for?

....

Q2. Complete the paragraph about industry in the NICs.

In recent years there has been a rapid growth of industry in the area of Asia called the

P............ R................ in countries such as S................ K................, T................,

H................ K................ and S........................... These four are called the four

t................ because they became so powerful and were in fierce competition with the older

manufacturing nations such as the U................ S................ and B................

Today they produce many goods, e.g. clothing, steel, cars, and electronics.

Q3. Describe <u>briefly</u> how each factor below helped industrial development in the NICs.

a) Labour ....

....

b) Government support and investment in infrastructure ....

....

c) The Asian market ....

....

d) Investment by multinational companies (such as Sony from Japan)

....

....

e) Strong leadership of NIC firms by clever businessmen.
Use particular companies to help explain your answer.
(Hint: South Korean companies — D..., Hy... and S...)

....

....

The NICs

Q4. Look at the pie charts for South Korea and answer the questions that follow.

Pie charts showing the % of people in Korea employed in the different types of industry

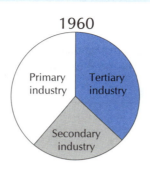
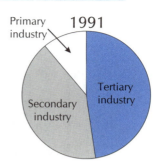

a) Approximately what proportion of the working population worked in primary industry in 1960? Circle the correct answer.

　　One half　　　One third　　　One quarter

b) Describe how this had changed by 1991.

　　..

　　..

c) What happened to the % of workers in manufacturing between 1961 and 1991? Circle the correct answer.

　　It halved　　　It doubled　　　It trebled

d) What has happened to the % in services over these 30 years?

　　..

　　..

e) In 1961, services meant mostly shops and the armed forces. Suggest two types of services which have now increased as a result of the increase in manufacturing.

　　1. ....

　　2. ....

Q5. Which basic factor in the location of industry was almost non-existent in the NICs?

　　..

Practise NICs — nick a few marks, hoho...

Like I said, the examiners (being the kind of people they are) love to test whether you understand the differences between an LEDC and an NIC. So make sure you can explain it. Then look around you for things made by Pacific Rim NICs — just so you get an idea of how important they are.

Section Four — Industry

Changing Industry — MEDCs

This is almost interesting because Britain is an MEDC. And so this is almost like a bit of history about this country. And it's fun too. Almost.

Q1. Use the graph to answer the questions which follow:

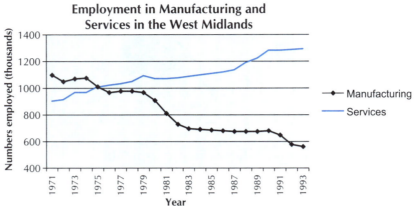

a) Which employed more people in 1971 – manufacturing or services? ....

b) What happens on the graph in 1975? ....

c) What then happened to the numbers employed in manufacturing? ....
....

d) What happened to the numbers employed in services? ....
....

Q2. Answer these questions about the recent trend in MEDCs for employment to "shift" from manufacturing to services.

a) Give <u>two</u> reasons why it has happened.

1. ....

2. ....

b) Circle the <u>five</u> service industries in the list below.

steelworks   banks   doctors   furniture makers   teachers   solicitors
dairy farmers   clothing manufacturers   police

c) Name <u>four</u> of the old traditional industries of Britain that have now declined.

1. ....   3. ....

2. ....   4. ....

d) Name an example of an old manufacturing site that has changed to services. (It could be a retail park or a tourist area now.)

....

Section Four — Industry

Changing Industry — MEDCs

Q3. This bar chart shows the % of the workforce employed in primary, secondary and tertiary/quaternary industry in Britain. Complete the chart by filling in the key.

Q4. Circle the <u>correct</u> word in each pair to finish this paragraph about industrial location.

Many old industries of the south/north have declined, eg chocolate/steel in Sheffield. Being near to local raw materials is/is not now a main location factor. Foreign raw materials can easily be imported/exported, so that ports have manufacturing industries such as foods and metals in Swansea, South Wales. Today many industries are called footloose/screwloose, which means that they can locate where they wish/within walking distance for people. They are usually near houses/roads and near the markets/raw materials.

Q5. Answer these questions about science parks.

a) What is a "science park"? ....
....

b) Name <u>three</u> industries that are found on science parks.

1. .... 2. .... 3. ....

c) Are these industries primary, secondary or tertiary? ....

d) Describe <u>three</u> important location factors for a science park.

1. .... 2. ....

3. ....

e) Are these industries traditional or footloose? Explain your answer.

....

Industry changes — if it didn't, you'd still be working in t' mill...

It's fascinating, isn't it. Absolutely fascinating. All this stuff about MEDCs — wonderful. And even if you don't think that, you still have to learn it. So, learning boots on and away you go.

Section Four — Industry

Multinational Companies

These multinational companies (MNCs) can also be called
TNCs (Transnational Corporations or Companies). Jargon, jargon everywhere...

Q1. Define an MNC. ....

....

Q2. Read this account of Unilever and then answer the questions.

Unilever is one of the world's largest industrial companies. Its headquarters are in Britain and Holland, where most of the manufacturing and research and development are located. The raw materials come from LEDCs all over the world, e.g. tea from India and palm oil from Zaire. There are processing factories too in the LEDCs, making use of the large, cheap labour force and the local market. Unilever's factories produce many foods and chemicals, e.g. margarine, ice cream, soap and detergents. They own many famous names such as Flora. They have a very large share of world trade and world agriculture and employ many people in plantations and factories in many host countries.

a) In which MEDCs are the parent companies for Unilever?
....

b) Why does the research and development go on in the parent countries?
....

c) Define "host country".
....

d) Name two of Unilever's host countries. Are these MEDCs or LEDCs?

1. ....

2. ....

e) Give three reasons why these have become host countries.

1. ....

2. ....

3. ....

MNC — easy as TNC... *(easy as Do Re Mi and CGP, baby you and me, oh baby now MNC...)*
These companies are extremely powerful — and that's what makes them worth knowing about.

Section Four — Industry

Section Five — Managing Resources

Use and Abuse of Resources

"Every act of destruction is an act of creation" or so Picasso once said — whether or not burning fossil fuels is art is between you and the dead painter, just make sure you can do these questions.

Q1. Define "sustainable development".

....

....

Q2. Define "renewable resources" and give three examples:

....

1. .... 2. .... 3. ....

Q3. Define "non-renewable resources" and give three examples:

....

1. .... 2. .... 3. ....

Q4. Answer these questions about fossil fuels.

a) Why are they called fossil fuels?

....

b) Name three fossil fuels.

1. .... 2. .... 3. ....

c) The burning of fossil fuels causes two problems:

A.............. r.................. and g.................. w..................

Q5. Fill in these examples of how the environment has been damaged by the abuse (the overuse) of the earth's resources.

a) The growing world population has led to increasing demands for f............ and w................

b) The over-use of the farmland leads to s............ e............ and des................

c) The ruthless demands for timber have led to de........................ and f..................

d) Mining and quarrying damage hab................ and create eye................

Use and Abuse of Resources

Q6. LEDCs often destroy large areas of trees (deforestation) e.g. in Kenya and Nepal.

a) Give <u>two</u> reasons why they need to use so many trees for fuel.

1. ....
2. ....

b) Describe <u>two</u> environmental problems that result from this deforestation.

1. ....
2. ....

Q7. Read this account of quarrying on the Isle of Portland, near Weymouth, Dorset and then answer the questions.

> The Isle of Portland is very scarred by limestone quarries. There are huge crater-like holes and piles of waste rock. Some of the residents have jobs in the quarrying industry, but they all have to put up with the noisy lorries, dusty air and damaged landscape. However the waste rock is useful – to protect the foot of the cliffs from coastal erosion. Also geology students can study the rocks exposed in the disused quarries.

a) What rock is quarried on the Isle of Portland? ....

b) Describe three ways in which the industry has damaged the island. Give one word answers.

1. .... 2. .... 3. ....

c) Describe three benefits (advantages) quarrying has brought. Give one word answers.

1. .... 2. .... 3. ....

d) Suggest one way in which disused quarries can often be a benefit to the environment.

....

Q8. Answer these questions about the conservation and recycling of resources:

a) Name two things that people can do to their homes to reduce their needs for heating fuel.

1. .... 2. ....

b) Name two farming techniques which reduce soil erosion.

1. .... 2. ....

Get up you stinking horrible useless excuse for a resource...

Lots of examples here, fossil fuels, deforestation, soil erosion, recycling, quarrying... the list is endless. Humans are always using resources but recently we've realised that we need to control this use, especially non-renewable resources — because, when they're gone, they're gone.

Energy and Power

"I have the power" — or so said He-Man, right before he did that transforming thing. Remember. OK you probably don't, but I'm reliving my youth here — let me have my fun...

Q1. The picture shows an <u>alternative</u> source of energy.

  a) Name this source.
  ....

  b) Circle the **two** types of areas which would be suitable for these machines.

   very steep slopes

   exposed lowland coastal areas

   fairly flat mountain tops

   deep valleys

Q2. We have been using <u>nuclear power</u> in Britain since the 1950s.

  a) Name a nuclear fuel.
  ....

  b) Do nuclear power stations need large or small quantities of this fuel?
  ....

  c) Name <u>two</u> important site factors for the location of a nuclear power station.

   1. ....
   2. ....

  d) Complete the table describing the advantages and disadvantages of nuclear power. Use the hints around the table to help you.

...carbon dioxide and sulphur dioxide...

Accidents...(eg?)

Amounts of fuel...

Waste...

Employment

Efficiency...

Nearby residents...

Leaks...

Advantages	Disadvantages

Section Five — Managing Resources

Energy and Power

Q3. Complete the notes to show how hydroelectric power is produced.

① A .... is built across a deep v................. in an area of h............ im........................ rock.

② The large deep r..................... provides the "head" of water. The water pressure at the b..................... of the dam is very high.

③ The water flows with great f..................... through pipes to the power house.

④ The fast flowing water turns the t........................... to g........................ the electricity.

⑤ Electricity is taken to towns and industry using p........................

Q4. Answer these questions about different sources of energy.

a) Iceland uses geothermal energy. Explain what geothermal energy is.
....

b) Some villages in India produce power from biomass. Explain what biomass is.
....

c) Tidal power is harnessed by building a barrage across an estuary. Suggest <u>two</u> disadvantages of building a barrage across the Severn estuary.
1. ....
2. ....

Q5. Complete these three sentences. In the future, planners need to...

a) protect the e........................   b) develop new t........................

c) make our use of energy more e........................

Q6 Describe <u>two</u> ways in which energy could be conserved in your school and/or home.
1. ....
2. ....

A teletubby suit — Po-wear...

Lots of types of power, all with pros and cons — makes for a lot to learn. But it's pretty important and it's also the kind of topic that you might have very strong views about — but you still have to know all sides of the subject so that you can make a balanced argument in the Exam.

Section Five — Managing Resources

Acid Rain

Some damage has already been done by our use of resources. Stand by for a few pages of bad news...

Q1. Define "acid rain". ....

Q2. Annotate the diagram to show how acid rain is formed.

1 ....
....
....

2 ....
....
....
....

3 ....
....
....
....

4 ....
....
....
....
....

Q3. Explain why pollution from Canada causes acid rain in Britain and Britain's pollution is causing acid rain in Scandinavia.

....

....

Q4. What are the effects of acid rain? Write about the following:

a) The effects on plants ....
....

b) The effects on rivers and lakes. ....
....

c) The effects on soil and crops. ....
....

d) What happens in ditches and streams as a knock-on effect of c)?
....
....

Q5. Look at the diagrams which show ways of reducing acid rain formation. Write notes by each diagram to explain what is going on.

....

....

Section Five — Managing Resources

Global Warming

Global warming sounds like quite a good idea when you're fed up of English weather, right? Wrong, because when the temperature patterns change it can cause serious problems...

Q1. What is meant by "global warming"?

....

....

....

Q2. By how much has the Earth's <u>average</u> temperature risen in the last 100 years? ....

Q3. Annotate the diagram to show the causes of global warming.

1. The burning of the r.......... f............ releases the gases .... and .... into the air.

2. Cleared areas no longer use up the gas c........................ in photo........................ .

3. The burning of f............ f............ release c........................ into the air.

4. Cars burn f............ f............ too.

5. The sun's rays pass through the a........................ and warm the earth.

6. But heat from earth cannot escape through the pollution, and so the t........................ rises.

Q4. The atmosphere has always acted like a blanket to keep in some of the heat, but human activities have increased the amounts of the gases which trap heat.

a) What name do we give to these gases? ....

b) Why is this name used?

....

c) Name two of these gases. 1. .... 2. ....

Section Five — Managing Resources

Global Warming

Q5. Answer these questions about the effects of global warming:

a) What is happening to the polar ice? ....

b) Have the last twenty years been the coldest or warmest on record? ....

c) What is happening to sea levels? ....

d) Give two reasons why this is happening.

1. ....

2. ....

e) What will be the impact (effect) of sea level change on Bangladesh?

....

f) Name four other places that will be affected like this.

1. ....   3. ....

2. ....   4. ....

Q6. Look at the world map of some possible effects of global warming, and answer the questions.

a) What may happen to the climate in the Caribbean? ....

b) Describe two knock-on problems which may result from this.

1. ....

....

2. ....

Drier:- fall in crop yields
Wetter climate, more flooding
More destructive hurricanes
More rain, farming may increase

c) What may happen in the Sahara? ....

d) The interior of the USA, Canada and Asia may become drier. What might this do to farming?

....

e) What may happen to rice farming in SE Asia? ....

....

f) How might this affect the people? ....

....

Section Five — Managing Resources

Pollution

Acid rain and global warming are the big well known examples of pollution. But the bad news doesn't stop there, there's air pollution, water pollution...

Q1. Give a brief definition of "pollution". ....
....

Q2. Give a brief definition of "environment". ....
....

Q3. Explain how the following cause air pollution, naming some of the gases.

   a) Power stations. ....
   ....

   b) Vehicles. ....
   ....

   c) Farm chemicals. ....
   ....

   d) Burning trees. ....
   ....

Q4. Look at the map of the River Rhône in France. Describe four different ways in which the river may become polluted and include, from the map, the name of a place for each one.

1. ....
....

2. ....
....

3. ....
....

4. ....

Map labels: Lyon; There are industrial towns; The Rhône is a tourist attraction with boats; Orange; Avignon; Mediterranean Sea; There are many towns & cities built along the Rhône; Areas growing vines and fruit

Section Five — Managing Resources

Pollution

Q5. Join (with a straight line) each type of pollution to the correct example of sea pollution.

a) Pollution from industrial chemicals.   THE MEDITERRANEAN SEA.

b) Oil spills and oil slicks.   THE EXXON VALDEZ, 1989, ALASKA.

c) Sewage.   THE COAST OF NORTH EAST ENGLAND.

Q6. Look at these sentences about land pollution. Match the muddled up halves by writing the answer in the spaces under the sentences.

a) Farming pollutes the land
b) Mining and quarrying pollute the land
c) Industry pollutes the land
d) Ordinary people pollute the land

1) by being ugly and creating spoil heaps.
2) with pesticides and fertilisers.
3) with dustbin rubbish and litter.
4) with ugly buildings and toxic waste.

a) matches ....   b) matches ....   c) matches ....   d) matches ....

Q7. Describe two types of areas where noise pollution is a problem.

1. ....   2. ....

Q8. And there are even more types of pollution:

a) What do we call the kind of pollution which spoils the scenery, eg by ugly scrapheaps, pylons and factories? ....

b) What do we call the kind of pollution caused by hot water? ....

Q9. Answer these questions about eutrophication, one of the results of river pollution.

a) Define "eutrophication" ....
....

b) Complete the notes in the boxes.

1. Rain falls on crop fields and ....

2. Some of the rain ....

3. In the streams ....

4. The water becomes starved of oxygen because ....
and this causes ....

Section Five — Managing Resources

National Parks

In the good old days we all ran around the countryside with only a loin cloth and sharpened stone for protection. Now we live in a concrete jungle, but thankfully we still have national parks... *

Q1. What is meant by a "National Park"? ....

....

Q2. Answer these questions about National Parks:

a) What is the name of the body which runs and looks after a National Park?

....

b) Fill in these three descriptions of the three jobs (or "Aims") of these bodies:

1. To protect the en..........................

2. To promote the public's enj.......................... and under.......................... of the park.

3. To look after the interests of the res..........................

c) Explain why it is not easy to be 100% successful in all three of these aims.

....

....

....

d) Difficulties or arguments which occur between different groups of people in the National Parks are known as c.......................... .

e) The first British National Parks were set up in 1951. Describe how transport and accessibility have changed since then.

....

....

f) List six problems which have occurred in the Parks as a result of these changes.

....

....

Q3. Use this chart to answer the questions about National Park land use:

The Overall Land Use in Britain's National Parks

- Moorland
- Farmland
- Woods and Forestry
- Other

a) What is the dominant (main) type of land use? ....

b) Does this make up ¼, ⅓ or ½ of the total? ....

c) What is the 2nd most important type of land use? ....

d) Roughly what proportion is woods and forestry? ....

e) A tiny amount of land is "other" land uses. Suggest two land uses that are classed as other.

1. .... 2. ....

Section Five — Managing Resources *CGP denies all responsibility for people arrested for running naked through National Parks.

National Parks

Q4. Answer <u>YES</u> or <u>NO</u> to these questions.

a) Is it easy to get permission to build a big, brightly coloured café within a National Park? ....

b) Are all developments strictly controlled? ....

c) Is mining and quarrying allowed? ....

d) Are National Parks owned by the Government? ....

e) Do people live in the British National Parks? ....

f) Is the name for a very popular tourist spot a "Money Pot"? ....

Q5. Look at the diagram which is called a <u>Conflict Matrix</u>. It shows which activities can cause problems for each other (eg by noise, litter or damage) and which do not.

Complete the matrix, by putting a tick where there may be conflict and a cross where there is not.

	Farming	Forestry	Walkers	Car trips	Coach Trips
Farming	X				
Forestry		X			
Walkers			X		
Car Trips				X	
Coach tours					X

X means no conflict
✓ means conflict

Q6. Look at the map of the Yorkshire Dales National Park.

a) Which cities do visitors to the Dales come from?

....

....

b) Roughly how many visitors come to the Dales each year?

....

c) Name two activities enjoyed by the visitors.

1. .... 2. ....

d) Describe and explain two environmental problems that occur at the honey pot sites.

1. ....

....

2. ....

....

e) Suggest one way of reducing the problem of too many cars in the Dales.

....

Oi — you in the loin cloth, get back here...

Who would have thought a little thing like National Parks could cause such conflict. But every time people want to use resources in different ways it's bound to happen. The main thing is... you've guessed it — understand both sides of the conflicts and think about sustainable solutions. Easy.

Section Five — Managing Resources

Tourism and Conflict

Tourism relies on a country's resources, both human and physical. But this creates pressure on the resources and conflict as to how they should be used...

Q1. Tourist destinations supply various <u>resources</u> for tourists.
Sort these resources into human resources and physical (natural) resources.

Hot sunshine; museums; art galleries; snow; restaurants; churches; waterfalls; wildlife; famous buildings; beaches.

<u>Human Resources</u>   <u>Physical Resources</u>

1) ....   1) ....

2) ....   2) ....

3) ....   3) ....

4) ....   4) ....

5) ....   5) ....

Q2. Match up each of these resources to one tourist destination by drawing a line between them:

a) Buildings, museums, entertainment   KENYA

b) Mountains and snow   SWITZERLAND

c) Wildlife and scenery   THE BAHAMAS

d) Hot sun and sandy beaches   LONDON

Q3. Answer these questions about <u>conflicts</u> and tourist demands in MEDCs.
For each one, explain the conflicts or problems:

Perhaps the conflict over the sun lounger had gone too far

a) Roads, toilets, car parks and cafes are provided for visitors.
But conservationists say ....
....
....

b) Tourists want to see attractive scenery, unspoilt by buildings and quarries.
But the residents say ....
....
....

Section Five — Managing Resources

Tourism and Conflict

Q3. continued...

c) Tourists want to walk, ride and picnic wherever they can.

But farmers say ....

....

....

d) Tourists want cruisers and water skiing on lakes (eg in the Lake District).

But walkers and fishermen say ....

....

....

Q4. Describe <u>three</u> types of conflict that can occur between local farmers, tourists and the environment in LEDCs.

1. ....
2. ....
3. ....

Q5. Describe <u>two</u> ways in which there can be conflict between the culture of the local people and the culture of the tourists in LEDCs.

1. Dress ....

....

2. Behaviour ....

....

Q6. Tourism can change the culture of LEDCs in other ways.
Tick T for True, or F for false, against each of these sentences.

	T	F	
a)	☐	☐	People in LEDCs often copy the tourists' style of clothes, eg jeans in Morocco.
b)	☐	☐	LEDCs are content to be poorer than MEDCs.
c)	☐	☐	MEDC tourists are all willing to eat the local foods.
d)	☐	☐	Many MEDC tourists demand Western-style drinks and menus.
e)	☐	☐	MEDC tourists all bother to learn the language of the LEDC they visit.

Toilet? T-O-I-L-E-T!? — cultural awareness — makes ya proud...

I like walking in the hills, but farmer Billy likes chasing me with a gun, yelling, 'get orf my laand'. That is an example of tourism causing conflict. Everywhere where people want to use resources in different ways there is conflict — you must understand these conflicts and how they can be managed.

Section Five — Managing Resources

Tourism in LEDCs

Tourism is a valuable source of income for many LEDCs. However it's not without its problems. It's the usual story, you need to understand all the pros and cons, so get into these...

Q1. Read this account of tourism in Goa, a state in South West India. Then answer the questions.

The disadvantages of tourism in Goa.

Tourism in Goa began in the 1960s. Goa was advertised as a hot, sunny paradise, with beautiful beaches and an interesting, exotic culture. Multi-storey hotels were built along the coast, destroying sand dunes and habitats. Local fishermen have lost their access to the beach. Sewage from the hotels and oil from pleasure boats has polluted the local rivers and the sea. Local people have lost their farmland, where foreign tourist companies have created golf courses. There are concerns about water shortages because the hotels use so much, whilst the locals do not even have a piped water supply. Hotel rubbish tips are often near villages. A lot of the profits of tourism go abroad to the tourism companies. In Goa this has made the gulf between rich tourists and poor locals more noticeable.

a) Describe five ways in which tourism in Goa has damaged the environment.

1. ....
2. ....
3. ....
4. ....
5. ....

b) Describe four ways in which the locals are treated as less important than the visitors.

1. ....
2. ....
3. ....
4. ....

c) What happens to most of the profits? ....

d) Why is this a problem for Goa? ....
....

e) Circle the word out of these two which you think describes the tourism in Goa.

    SUSTAINABLE   EXPLOITATION

Holiday in India — let's go(a)...

It's hard to imagine that there can be problems with lounging around on a beach, enjoying a new culture and sipping a coke. But what about the rubbish, what about the people who are trying to live their normal lives — when you think about it it's lucky you're stuck answering geography questions.

Section Five — Managing Resources

Section Six — Development

Measuring Development

This section is full of abbreviations that you've seen before. Now it's time to check you understood what you were talking about — and learn some more detail as well — you love it...

Q1. These are measures of development. Give a definition of each (and say what they stand for).

a) GDP per capita ....
....

b) GNP ....
....

c) Life Expectancy ....
....

d) Infant Mortality Rate ....
....

Q2. Name and define one other measure of development — "development index".
....
....

Q3. Look at this graph and answer the questions which follow.

a) What is a graph like this called? ....

b) Are the group A countries MEDCs or LEDCs? ....

c) Are the group B countries MEDCs or LEDCs? ....

d) Which group would Britain be in — A or B? ....

e) Explain carefully what this graph is showing. (Don't just copy the labels on the axes.)
....
....

f) What kind of correlation is shown? ....

Measuring development — geography topic, or a snazzy new ruler...
Lots of tricky terms to remember — difficult. But you've definitely got to know them. Bummer.

Contrasts in Development

By measuring development, you can see that some countries are more developed than others.
Is this fun or what... well, it's not fun but it does contain lots of geography questions — like you'd expect.

Q1. Answer the following questions.

a) Circle the three countries below which are considered to be 'rich'.

    Ethiopia   USA   Zimbabwe   Peru   Australia   Britain

b) Are these richer countries known as MEDCs or LEDCs?

....

c) What do the letters MEDC and LEDC stand for?

    MEDC: ....

    LEDC: ....

d) Give two other names for the LEDCs.

    1. ....   2. ....

Q2. Look at the bar charts. Which one (A, B or C) shows the MEDCs of the world?

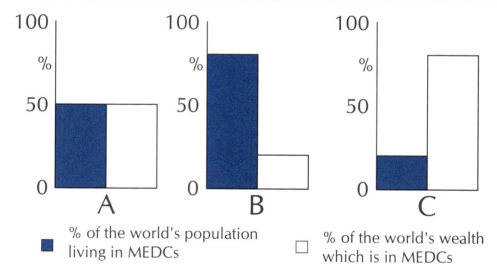

■ % of the world's population living in MEDCs
□ % of the world's wealth which is in MEDCs

Q3. Fill in this definition of "development".

A country which is more developed has a high st................ of l................ .
The people earn a good income from jobs in p................, s................,
t................ or q................ industry. The country is well served by
services such as tr................ t, ed................ n, he................ th
and lei................ re.

Section Six — Development

Contrasts in Development

Q4. Answer these questions about countries which used to be LEDCs (like South Korea).

a) These countries are now called something else.
   Give the new three-letter abbreviation and what it stands for.

   ....

b) Name <u>two</u> more of these countries.

   1. .... 2. ....

Q5. Answer these questions about the 'development gap'.

a) What is meant by the 'development gap'?

   ....

b) What is meant by "The north-south divide"?

   ....

Q6. Look at the map.

a) Draw on a line to mark the north-south divide.

b) In which hemisphere are the richer countries? Circle the correct answer.

           The northern hemisphere   The southern hemisphere

c) What <u>two</u> countries are exceptions to this rule?

   1. .... 2. ....

Chilli con carne, development contrast — <u>not v. similar...</u>

If you remember one thing from these two pages, remember what <u>MEDC</u> and <u>LEDC</u> stand for. You <u>will</u> get asked questions with them in — they crop up in most of the human geography topics (and in physical geography too). Don't muddle them. Not even sometimes. Keep going over 'em.

Section Six — Development

Environmental Problems and Development

LEDCs often have natural problems to contend with.
Know what they are and the effects they can have.

Q1. The diagram shows four environmental problems that make development in LEDCs difficult. Name the four problems.

a) C............e   b) D............e

c) P............s   d) N............ D............rs

Q2. Write down the LEDCs which match each sentence (a to e) describing climate problems which slow down development.

Nigeria   India   Sudan   Bangladesh   The Bahamas   Nepal

a) The area around the Sahara is hot with unreliable rain and frequent droughts making food production difficult. ....

b) Water supply is often a problem. ....

c) Soil erosion is common when people try to farm steep slopes in areas of heavy rainfall. ....

d) Flooding makes life very difficult in lowlands in monsoon areas. ....

e) Death and damage occurs more often in the tropics due to hurricanes. ....

f) Attempts to build roads are often ruined by the heavy tropical rains. ....

Q3. Answer these questions about the many diseases found in the tropics which make development in LEDCs difficult.

a) Name the main disease spread by the mosquito. ....

b) Name a disease carried in water by snails. ....

c) Name a disease that people catch by drinking polluted water. ....

It's the end of the world as we know it — great, no more exams...

It rains a bit in Britain. BIG DEAL. They get proper bad weather in some places in the world — bad enough to interfere with farming and industry and stuff. You've gotta know what the weather problems are, and where they happen. (Alright, it floods sometimes here, but they get much much worse floods in Bangladesh.)

Section Six — Development

Dependency and the Colonial Past

For some reason, Britons (and other people) of the past roamed the world taking over foreign countries. That led to problems in the development of those countries, and there are still some problems today...

Q1. Many LEDCs used to be *colonies* of MEDCs, eg India used to be ruled by Britain.

a) What kind of goods did the colonies supply to MEDCs — raw materials or manufactured goods?

....

b) Why did the MEDCs want these?

....

c) What kind of goods did the MEDCs sell to the colonies?

....

d) Why did this slow down the development of the colonies?

....

....

e) Why did the colonial rulers not help the colonies to set up their own secondary industries?

....

....

f) The colonies had to rely on the MEDCs. This is described as D............................cy.

g) Today, many former colonies are still being used by MEDCs, as host countries for MNCs. What is an MNC, and how do they operate?

....

....

....

h) Name an example of:

1) An MNC .... 2) The owner country ....

3) One of its host countries .... 4) One of its products ....

Britain used to run America — funny how things change...

Weird. In the Victorian age <u>one third</u> of the world was run by Britain. And France and Spain had colonies too. So now there are lots of countries with the types of problems mentioned on this page.

Section Six — Development

International Trade

International Trade is one of the big issues of our times. I bet you're wearing something right now that was made abroad. And if it's a big issue, you can bet it'll be big in exams too.

Q1. Complete this definition of trade:

"Trade is the e............ of g............ and s............ between countries."

Q2. Define imports and exports.

a) Imports: ....

b) Exports: ....

Q3. What kind of goods make up most of the LEDCs' exports – raw materials or manufactured goods?

....

Q4. Name <u>four</u> examples of this type of goods.

1. ....   3. ....

2. ....   4. ....

Q5. What kind of goods make up most of the MEDCs' exports?

....

Q6. Name <u>four</u> examples of this type of goods that Britain exports.

1. ....   3. ....

2. ....   4. ....

Q7. Correct this paragraph by circling the right words in the pairs:

<u>The disadvantages of relying on the export of raw materials (primary products).</u>
Raw materials are sold for much higher/lower prices than manufactured goods. The prices are fixed by the LEDCs/MEDCs. The price for raw materials varies/does not vary from year to year (eg for crops it depends on how good the harvest is). Some countries have suffered because man-made substances now partly replace natural raw materials eg Malaysian rice/rubber plantations suffered due to the invention of plastics and India's exports of cotton/cuckoo clocks declined as a result of the invention of man-made fibres.

Section Six — Development

International Trade

Q8. Look at the graph and answer the questions.

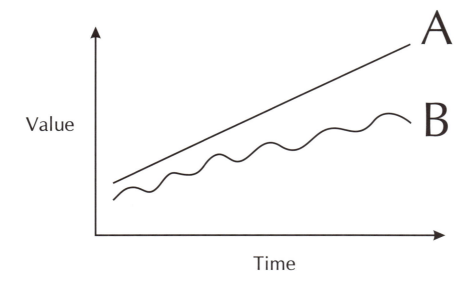

a) One line on this graph shows the prices of manufactured goods and the other shows the prices of raw materials.

Which line is A?

....

Which line is B?

....

b) Which goods always have a higher value?

....

c) Which goods fluctuate more in price through time?

....

d) Why does the answer to c) make things difficult for LEDCs?

....

e) Describe what is happening to the two lines through time, and explain what this means for the "development gap".

Through time: ....

This means: ....

Section Six — Development

International Trade

Q9. Define "Trade Bloc".

....

....

a) Examples of Trade Blocs are the EU, OPEC and NAFTA. What do these letters stand for?

EU ....

OPEC ....

NAFTA ....

b) Explain how Trade Blocs protect and encourage trade within the group of member countries.

....

....

c) Explain how Trade Blocs make it difficult for LEDCs to compete with MEDCs' manufacturing industry.

....

....

Q10. Some countries which used to be LEDCs did manage to compete so that they became important manufacturing countries. Their governments helped their industrial growth and made imported products more expensive.

a) What are these countries now called? (Give the letters, and say what the letters stand for).

....

....

b) The <u>four</u> Asian countries which are examples of the above are:

1. ....   2. ....

3. ....   4. ....

c) Name <u>two</u> examples of manufactured goods that Britain imports from any of these countries.

1. ....   2. ....

Two sheckels for that goat? — it's hardly worth one, look at its ears...

As with most things in life Henry, international trade is great, and it's bad, both at the same time. You've got to know the pros and cons well enough to scribble them down in the <u>exam</u> — use these questions as <u>valuable practice</u>. ...Never forget that trade can include <u>services</u> as well as goods.

Section Six — Development

The Question of Aid

Countries like Britain often send aid to poorer places, especially if there's been a disaster like a flood or an earthquake. There are different types of aid, and you need to know all about it.

Q1. Why do some countries need aid?

....

....

Q2. Which countries are the most likely to need aid — the LEDCs or the MEDCs?

....

Q3. Explain what is meant by each of the following:

a) Bi-lateral aid ....

....

b) Multi-lateral aid ....

....

c) Non-governmental aid ....

....

d) Tied aid ....

....

Q4. Describe, using a case study that you have studied, an example of aid.

....

....

....

....

Section Six — Development

The Question of Aid

Q5. Fill in the table to show <u>four</u> reasons why aid is a good idea and <u>four</u> reasons why it is not. Include examples.

<u>Positives</u>	<u>Negatives</u>
1	1 ....
2	2 ....
3	3 ....
4	4 ....

Q6. If a country has a food supply problem, which of the following types of aid do you think Britain should send? Tick the one you choose.

A ☐ Money.

B ☐ Food supplies.

C ☐ Trained workers to help set up self-help village schemes.

D ☐ Workers and money to set up large-scale agricultural projects with irrigation and fertilisers.

Explain why you have chosen this one, and then explain why you did not choose each of the other three.

I chose scheme ...., because ....

....

I did not choose ...., because ....

....

I did not choose ...., because ....

....

I did not choose ...., because ....

....

Comic relief — I'll stop writing these jokes...

Don't start thinking that all aid is the same — it isn't. Working out exactly what to send is the hardest part — you've got to think of the long term as well as the short term. Not easy. And you've got to know it for the exam. Great. Read through the Revision Guide if you're not sure.

Section Six — Development

Development Projects

One of the best forms of aid is to set up <u>development projects</u> — helping people to help themselves.

Q1. Correct this paragraph about development projects by circling the correct words in the pairs.

Small-scale projects, eg the digging of a well/the building of a dam, are designed to help large/small numbers of people. Local people/foreign technicians are trained to run the projects and money comes from the Government/Bingo and from charities such as Oxfam and the Blue Peter appeals. Any schemes are designed to be run by MNCs/self-sufficient.

Q2. What other name is often given to these types of small-scale projects?

....

Q3. Circle the correct description of such small projects.

Quaternary Industry   Appropriate Technology   Dependency

Q4. Fill in these descriptions of the different types of small-scale projects.

a) Some projects provide basic necessities of life for the people, eg clean .... and san .... schemes.

b) Some projects provide services to improve the people's lives, eg they provide a cl............ or a sch ....

c) Some projects help people with their money and savings by ....
....

Q5. Describe <u>two</u> advantages and <u>two</u> disadvantages of large scale development projects compared with short scale development projects.

Advantages: ....
....
....

Disadvantages: ....
....
....

For development-project-fish-analogy, see below...
"Give someone a fish, and you'll feed their family tonight.
Teach someone to make fishing rods, and they'll feed their family for a lifetime."   Nuff said.

Section Six — Development

Section Seven — Answers

Pages 1 – 13

Page 1

Q1 The way people are spread out throughout the world.
Q2 Japan; Bangladesh; NW Europe; E USA.
Q3 <u>Reasons why areas have many people:</u> climate is not extreme; lowland areas; rich industrial areas; fertile soils.
<u>Reasons why areas have few people:</u> desert areas; high mountainous areas; very cold areas; poor areas of rapid population growth.
Q4 Europe – it is a wealthy industrial area;
North Canada – it is cold and windy, with dark winters;
Bangladesh – it is fertile lowland with rapid population growth;
The Himalayas – it is too steep and cold for many crops and buildings.

Pages 2, 3

Q1 The number of people per unit area. eg per square km.
Q2 area
Q3 Distribution tells us where people live – and whether there are many or few. Density tells us the average number of people over the whole area, but does not tell us how they are spread out.
Q4 **a)** overpopulation or overpopulated. **b)** food; clean water; soil; oil and gas; houses. **c)** disease is very common. (other answers: could be not enough houses so there are lots of shanty towns; or starvation)
Q5 means that the area could have more people – at present there are plentiful resources and land, and not enough people to use them all. eg Australia.
Q6 optimum population.
Q7 **a)** south and east. **b)** 1. Highlands of Scotland; 2. The Pennines; 3. The Lake District (Cumbria); 4. Snowdonia; 5. Dartmoor.
c) remote areas with few jobs.
d) A ...Scotland ..Glasgow...Edinburgh.
B ...Newcastle....
C ...Liverpool and Manchester.
D ...coal....
E....Midlands
F ...London

Pages 4, 5

Q1 **a)** 0.4 billion
b) 0.8 billion
c) × 2
d) 6.4 billion
e) × 8
f) For centuries rates of world population growth were the same and very slow. Then there was a sudden increase in the rate in the late 18th century, so that in the last 3 centuries they have been very rapid.
Q2 **a)** the number of live babies born per thousand of the population, per year.
b) the number of deaths per thousand of the population, per year.
c) the numbers of people moving (migrating) into or out of the area.
Q3 Population explosion.
Q4 The Demographic Transition Model.
Q5 **a)** No birth control.
b) Disease, wars and starvation.
c) Death rate fell; reasons – better understanding of diseases and how to avoid them; improved living standards; better food; the start of vaccinations and better medicine.
d) It speeded up.
e) Low.
f) Rate of growth slowed right down to very low rate.

Pages 6, 7

Q1 ...age ...males ...females. ...young people/children. ...narrow (or thinner).
Q2 **a)** quite high; **b)** few; **c)** high; **d)** high; **e)** they must have moved away; **f)** A is Bombay   B is Eastbourne.
Q3 **a)** .....high ..... high   = pyramid B.
b) .....high   ..falling = pyramid D.
c) ...falling   = pyramid C.
d) ...low........low...   = pyramid A.
Q4 The numbers of babies who die before their first birthday, per thousand of the population per year.
Q5 correct answer is a).
Q6 The people who are aged 16 to 65, who can earn a living.

Pages 8

Q1 $\dfrac{\text{nos. of children up to 15} + \text{nos. of elderly of 65 and over}}{\text{nos. of economically active people}} \times 100$
Q2 Dependency Ratio = 50.
Q3 Correct words are: LEDCs; over 100; education; lots of; explosion; houses; over.
Q4 circle these- Doctors and hospitals; buses and trains; sheltered housing; nursing homes.
Q5 **a)** low....fall/decline.
b) economically active / working.
c) increases
Q6 **a)** MEDC **b)** LEDC.

Page 9, 10

Q1 **a)** birth rate
Q2 **b)** providing food
Q3 1) educating people about birth control 2) making contraception available (OR provide benefits for people with fewer children).
Q4 1) some religions eg Catholics in Mexico are against birth control.
2) some cultures encourage families to have many sons.
Q5 *unhealthy* children; *high* infant mortality; high birth *rate*.
Q6 India.
Q7 **a)** overpopulated; **b)** 1) poverty 2) poor health 3) famine (could have low life expectancy too). **c)** 1) poor health 2) not enough food; **d)** 1) people could not get permission to marry til age 22; 2) people could only have one child per family. **e)** 50%;
Q8 **Top row** Irrigation; MEDC – California or Colorado basin; LEDC India – water supplies are already a problem – this can lead to shortages; costly
2nd row MEDC – Holland; costly, loss of plants and wildlife.
3rd row Fertilisers; MEDC – Britain; costly, pollution of water with nitrates.
4th row Pesticides; MEDC – Britain; costly, can kill other species, eg bees, wildflowers.

Page 11

Q1 A migrant.
Q2 **a)** movements of people from one country to another country.
b) regional migration. **c)** local migration.
Q3 **a)** 1) cold wet climate 2) poor job opportunities. **b)** push factors.
c) 1) wonderful climate 2) better paid jobs. **d)** pull factors.

Page 12, 13

Q1 1) in search of better paid jobs 2) better education for their children 3) better standard of living.
Q2 **a)** warm sunny climate. **b)** job opportunities with higher pay.
c) the loss of highly educated and skilled people when they migrate away to other countries.

Pages 13 – 23

Q3 PUSH – farming is poor; few jobs; poor sanitation;
PULL – better education; more hospitals; place is busy & modern.

Q4 **a)** the move of people away from urban areas, to live in rural areas. **b)** commuting. **c)** cars.

Q5 **a)** 1) oppression because of their religion. 2) because of their race. (other ideas linked to fleeing from earthquake, volcanic or other disasters.) **b)** eg Jews fleeing Germany in World War 2.

Q6 Government could encourage transport links from quieter areas to the business centres. They could also encourage businesses to set up in the quieter areas with incentives like cheaper business rates. This will encourage people to move to these areas for work.

Q7 **a)** India to Britain. **b)** Britain to Australia. **c)** Mexican village to Mexico City. **d)** counterurbanisation eg from London to a village outside the city. **e)** refugees from Bosnia.

Page 14

Q1 A place where people live, such as a village or town.

Q2 The actual place in the physical landscape that the settlement is built on. Eg. on a hill.

Q3 Situation refers to a wider area, saying where the settlement is in relation to other settlements and how near it is to major roads, railways, an airport or a port. It refers to the human environment in the large area around the settlement.

Q4 Site factors are things that cause a settlement to be built in a particular place. They are reasons for the site. Eg water supply.

Q5 **a)** water supply. **b)** spring line settlements. **c)** 1) on a hill for defence against attack 2) a dry place above wet lands.
d) 1) crossing place on the river 2) a crossroads of routes.
e) safety or defence inside a meander loop. **f)** defensive **g)** B
h) B **i)** building materials eg wood; good soil for farming. (possible answer is wood for fuel.)

Page 15

Q1 C– City; T – Town; V – Village; H – Hamlet.

Q2 **a)** Services are things that settlements provide for people eg shops, banks. **b)** No. of services increases. **c)** Positive **d)** Post office; corner shop; infant school. **e)** Because villages only have a small population, therefore there are not enough people to make these others worthwhile or profitable. **f)** Low **g)** High order

Pages 16, 17

Q1 **a)** The area surrounding a settlement. The settlement provides shops and jobs for the people of this area. Also the area provides leisure activities, and farm produce for the settlement.
b) 1) Urban Field 2) Catchment Area 3) Market Area 4) Hinterland. **c)** Central Place
d) 1) services (eg a bank); 2) administration (eg the Council House); 3) employment (eg jobs in the hospital or shops).
e) 1) You could investigate the area served by the hospital or 2) the area to which the local paper is delivered or 3) the town's post delivery area.

Q2 Small, because it only has a few services, and they are low order (eg a small post office, with a small number of customers). People will only travel a short distance for these kind of services, making the sphere of influence small.

Q3 Large, because it has a lot of services, of low, middle and high order. People will travel further for the ones of the higher orders eg people are prepared to travel further to buy a coat or visit the dentist.

Q4 Correct words are: low; milk; short; bank; larger; seven; high; larger.

Q5 Christaller.
a) Because circles don't fit together (tessellate), whereas hexagons do.
b) Central Place Theory.

Pages 18, 19

Q1 **a)** 1. The CBD 2. Transition Zone and wholesale light manufacturing 3. Low quality residential 4. Medium quality residential 5. High quality residential. **b)** Burgess. **c)** the CBD. **d)** on the city edge.

Q2 **a)** The Sector Model. **b)** Hoyt. **c)** They are along roads and railways. **d)** The CBD.

Q3 Correct words are: heart; shopping; offices; high; multi-storey; a shortage; up; famous-name; high; very low.

Q4 **b)** is correct.

Q5 An area of countryside that has not yet had any development on it.

Q6 Dormitory villages.

Page 20

Q1 The process where more and more of the population of an area become town and city dwellers. The % of the total population that is urban increases.

Q2 **a)** LEDC cities are growing at a much faster rate. **b)** 1) rapid rural to urban migration 2) high birth rate in cities (because migrants are young).

Q3 **a)** elderly **b)** the elderly population is less able to do difficulty, physical work. **c)** invests little money **d)** the young have left and there are fewer
e) those of working age have left.

Page 21

Q1 The movement outwards of people from the city, to live in rural areas. It occurs in MEDCs.

Q2 1) Noise from traffic. 2) Air pollution (traffic, central heating, dust). 3) Overcrowding. 4) Rush hour congestion and stress.

Q3 The setting up of new business parks on the edge of cities has encouraged people to move outwards to live.

Q4 1) People can often buy a larger house and larger garden in rural areas where there is more space. 2) People often move out of a city when they retire, to live in a more peaceful area

Page 22, 23

Q1 **a)** 1) Factories have been unable to expand in the Inner City because of shortage of space and have moved to the city edge where land can be cheaper and access is easier. 2) Many factories have closed down due to foreign competition.
b) The areas look unattractive and uninviting to new investors. (other answers could be about: shortage of space; or difficulties of access by delivery lorries). **c)** Employment levels in the Inner City have fallen – there are more and more unemployed. **d)** Original houses are in a poor state, in need of repairs – this is because they are very old. **e)** Deprived means there is a great shortage of things that people need in order to have a good standard of living. Eg a shortage of jobs, shops, schools, parks, and people are often on low incomes. **f)** "Social amenities" are services that people need such as leisure activities like sports clubs; evening classes; nurseries and clinics.

Q2 1) Cars can use lead-free petrol. 2) By making public transport cheap, so that fewer people will use their cars.

Q3 Correct words are: The Government; Urban Renewal Schemes; With new housing; in light industry; more shops, clinics, sports facilities.

Q4 **a)** 1) overcrowding and shortage of space. 2) expensive sites. (another idea could be old unsuitable buildings).
b) 1) more space (for buildings and car parks) 2) more attractive, green environment.
c) Birmingham Business Park, near the airport in Birmingham.

Section Seven — Answers

Pages 23 – 32

d) 1) They are new, bright, modern, and under cover, out of the weather. 2) They are free of traffic – safer, quieter, no fumes. **e)** The Pavillions, in Birmingham.

Q5 The "Donut Effect", which started in USA.

Page 24, 25

Q1 **a)** near the edge. **b)** 1) long difficult journeys to work 2) high cost of commuting. (another answer could be creation of large traffic jams). **c)** 1) Near the CBD. 2) Along roads to the West and South West. **d)** Near roads and railways to the North and North East. **e)** 1) pollution 2) traffic congestion (another answer could be noise). **f)** 1) deforestation of the vegetation. 2) soil erosion. (another answer could be landslides).

Q2 Correct words are: rapidly; rural; on the edge; shortage; 1) water 2) waste 4) refuse (rubbish); 4) sewerage.

Q3 **a)** T; **b)** T; **c)** F; **d)** T; **e)** T; **f)** F.

Q4 A – 3; B – 4; C – 1; D – 2.

Page 26

Q1 **a)** The edge of the city, where the city meets the countryside. **b)** The unplanned growth of the city, spreading outwards.

Q2 1) To protect the countryside, and keep these areas as green areas. 2) To reduce traffic congestion especially at rush hours.

Q3 Counterurbanisation.

Q4 A conurbation is a large built-up area where several settlements have spread and joined together. Eg London; or The West Midlands conurbation (with Birmingham, Walsall, Dudley and other towns within it).

Q5 1) Golf courses, eg the Belfry near Birmingham. 2) Farms that have craft units and activities for children eg Hatton World, near Birmingham. 3) Areas of country walks eg the Lickey Hills, on the edge of Birmingham.

The Industry Section is kindly sponsored by Birmingham Tourism — *Birmingham, nearer than you'd think.*

Page 27

Q1 Agriculture is the production of crops and animals, for food and industry.

Q2 It is important because all people need food, and other products are made too such as clothing from cotton.

Q3 Primary.

Q4 **a)** 1) The climate is drier than in many parts of Britain, being in the rain shadow. (Rainfall 590 mm/year). Summers are warm and dry. 2) Soils are chalky, and alkaline, and are improved with organic matter from the farm. 3) The relief is flat and not very high, being 30 m above sea level. **b)** There are inputs of money (capital) eg to buy seeds and fertiliser; labour – 2 full time and 2 part time workers; special buildings and machinery have been provided. **c)** Outputs are beans, sugar beet, wheat and barley. **d)** 1) Profits from the sale of crops. 2) Seeds. **e)** 1) How much land to devote to each crop each year. 2) How many workers he needs and how much to pay them. 3) Which crop to grow in which field (crop rotation). (Other answers are possible eg when to plough, when to start planting, or should he buy any more machinery…..)

Pages 28, 29

Q1 Arable farms – They specialise in growing crops. Pastoral farms – They specialise in animal rearing. Mixed farms – They have both animals and crops.

Q2 **a)** Correct words are: high; high; in a market garden in Worcs; high, LEDCs. **b)** Correct words are: large; poor; few; a wheat farm in the Canadian Prairies.

Q3 **a)** A pesticide is a substance made of chemicals that destroys "pests" which are weeds or creatures that the farmer doesn't want. **b)** A fertiliser is made of chemicals (eg nitrates) and helps crops to grow well.

Q4 **a)** Subsistence farming. **b)** Commercial farming. **c)** The people clear a small plot, then cultivate it for a few years until the soil becomes exhausted. Then they leave it and move on, and clear another plot. **d)** Amazonia. **e)** Cash crops. **f)** Factory farming is when many animals are kept very close together, indoors, to produce as much output as possible. Eg Battery chickens.

Q5 **b)** An arable, intensive, commercial farm. **c)** A pastoral, extensive, commercial farm. **d)** An arable, intensive, commercial farm. **e)** An arable, intensive, commercial farm. **f)** An arable, intensive, subsistence farm. **g)** A pastoral, intensive, commercial farm.

Page 30

Q1 **a)** Arable farming occurs mostly in the East and South East of England. A lot of East Anglia has arable farms (eg in Norfolk). In the South East there are many arable farms eg in Sussex and Kent. Arable farming occurs in the lowlands of England. **b)** Sheep farming occurs mostly in the West, South West and the North. It occurs in areas of hills and mountains, such as Dartmoor and Exmoor in the South West, and in the hills of the North such as The Pennines and the Yorkshire Dales.

Q2 1) Climate 2) Relief 3) Soils.

Q3 Correct words are: hot; cold; commercial; arable; pastoral; mixed; intensive; extensive; MEDCs.

Pages 31, 32

Q1 The Common Agricultural Policy.

Q2 It guaranteed a set price to farmers for their products, even if too much was produced (which would normally make prices fall). Also it protected European farmers from cheap imports from outside the EU.

Q3 To increase farm output (yield). 2) To improve farm efficiency.

Q4 **First diagram** - The CAP led farmers to over-produce, which led to huge <u>surpluses</u> which were nicknamed the wheat, butter and meat mountains, and the wine and the milk lakes. These had to be stored, and eventually were destroyed. There was an outcry about the waste.
Second diagram – This diagram shows that farmers wanted to produce as much as possible, and so they made their farms more efficient, by removing hedges, making fields bigger, and using chemical pesticides and fertilisers. But all these things caused environmental damage. Soil erosion by wind occurred, and chemicals got into the water supply. Wild creatures and plants lost their habitats, and were killed by pesticides. Many species of insects, animals, plants and birds declined.

Q5 **a)** …Quota…. milk. **b)** …Set Aside Schemes…….crops. **c)** Diversification ………………….such as Bed and Breakfast (other possible answers include caravan sites, craft shops, stables and others). **d)** ….environment…..Environmentally Sensitive Areas.

Q6 **a)** They were paid money called a subsidy to encourage them to produce more. **b)** The Quota system was introduced, which set a limit on the amount that a farmer could produce, and he was fined if he over-produced. **c)** The man from the Ministry is saying: "You must reduce your milk production and if you exceed your new limit, you will be fined."
The farmer is saying "What if my herd increases? Do I have to sell my extra animals? Will the policy stay the same? How can I plan ahead?"

Pages 32 – 39

Q7 …..15% …..5 years…..subsidy

Q8 **a)** Diversification Schemes allow farmers to use some land for non-farming uses, and they can receive income from this.
b) 1) Horse riding and stabling. 2) Bed and Breakfast. 3) Craft shops. 4) Visitor centres eg for people to see rare breeds. Other answers are possible eg creating caravan sites.

Q9 **a)** 1. The Yorkshire Dales. 2. The Peak District. 3. The Norfolk Broads. 4. The South Downs.
b) Farmers are paid a subsidy if they farm in an environmentally friendly way – eg if they agree not to use chemicals, or if they return to the use of horses.

Page 33

Q1 **a)** 1. This is done for you. 2. Fields were smaller in 1945, and much bigger in 2001. 3. There were lots of hedgerows and trees in 1945. These were removed to make more room for crops, so that in 2001 there are few trees. 4. There are several workers, all working by hand in 1945. In 2001 it is very mechanised. 5. Animals are grazing out in the fields in 1945, but are raised indoors in 2001. 6. Jobs were slower and less efficient in 1945, and in 2001 machines made jobs faster and more efficient, with far fewer workers. 7. There is no sign of chemicals in 1945, but in 2001 chemicals are being sprayed in this case from an aeroplane. 8. The landscape is more natural and attractive in 1945, and in 2001 is unnatural, modern and business-like.
b) any reasonable answers, eg soil erosion, loss of habitats for hedgerow animals

Q2 Reasons for removing hedgerows: **1.** Removing hedges creates more space for crops, increasing the output. **2.** To create larger fields, which were needed in order to use the larger machinery (eg combine harvesters need a large space to turn in). **3.** Hedges need trimming, and can be home to pests and diseases.
Reasons why hedgerows are important:
1. They are attractive, with different species, flowers and berries.
2. They protect against the wind and soil erosion, and roots hold the soil in place. **3.** They are habitats for wildlife, providing homes and food.

Pages 34, 35

Q1 **a)** Subsistence. **b)** Low. **c)** Intensive. **d)** The rapid population increase. **e)** Shortage of suitable land on these steep slopes.
f) 1) soil erosion 2) landslides. (Deforestation is another answer).
g) The land is unsuitable for much agriculture, so that any attempts to increase their yields leads to soil exhaustion, erosion and collapse of the terraces in landslides.

Q2 1) Shifting cultivation in Amazonia. 2) The Tuaregs on the Sahara borders (in Sudan) who practise extensive pastoral subsistence farming (nomadic herding).

Q3 **a)** A plantation is a very large estate producing cash crops.
b) Commercial. **c)** 1) Rubber in Malaysia. 2) Tea in India. (Other answers possible eg coffee, or sugar cane in Brazil).
d) The growing of one crop only.

Q4 **a)** Tea and coffee. **b)** Multinational Companies. **c)** Abroad, to the MEDCs who own the companies. **d)** Local farmers have been forced off their land onto poorer land. **e)** This has caused soil erosion by wind (dry season) and rain (wet season). **f)** Marginal.

Q5 **a)** You name your case study of a plantation.
b) The Advantages of plantations: 1) They enable LEDCs to sell products abroad, and bring them some money. 2) They provide jobs for people in areas where people find it hard to get work.
3) More modern methods are used and the people are taught new skills.
The Disadvantages of plantations: 1) They are often monocultures which are affected by variations in world prices. Also hazards like drought, floods or pests can wipe out all the crop.
2) Labourers are poorly paid, and forced off their lands, making it difficult for them to produce their own food. 3) Most of the profits go abroad, and do not benefit the "host" country.

Pages 36, 37

Q1 **a)** F; **b)** T; **c)** T; **d)** F; **e)** F; **f)** T; **g)** T.

Q2 **a)** ……..rapid population growth. **b)** ……..yields.

Q3 HYVs are High Yielding Varieties of crops. They were produced by scientists, and are special seeds which raise the output of crops.

Q4 **a)** 1) wheat 2) maize. **b)** rice. **c)** 1) India 2) SE Asia eg. Malaysia.

Q5 The 4 ways are: **1)** They are dwarf varieties which can be grown closer together without shading out other plants, and which makes them less easily damaged by wind. **2)** They have smaller roots, make maximum use of fertiliser, and can be grown even if the soil is not itself very fertile. **3)** HYVs are disease-resistant. **4)** They have a shorter growing season, so that more than one crop can be grown each year.

Q6 The correct one is Appropriate technology.

Q7 **Successes:** Rice production has doubled. New farming methods have created new jobs…. Two crops per year are possible with irrigation. People are healthier. People have surplus food to sell and therefore have more money. There are new jobs in the factories ….
Failures: The use of machinery has caused farm workers to lose their jobs. Some farms are very small and farmers can't afford the new seeds and fertiliser. Many farm workers migrate to the cities….Poorer farmers are afraid to change….. Schemes for borrowing money are not well developed.

Pages 38, 39

Q1 **a)** Desertification is the spread of desert-like conditions into areas on the desert borders, caused by too much farming by too many people in unsuitable areas. **b)** Areas shown are: 1. The South West of USA, including the states of California, Arizona and New Mexico. 2. The North East of Brazil. 3. The interior of Argentina in South America. 4. Lands to the North of the Sahara Desert, eg Algeria. 5. Large areas to the South of the Sahara Desert, eg Ethiopia and Sudan. 6. Areas of South Africa, such as Namibia. 7. Parts of the Middle East. 8. Areas of Asia, such as Pakistan. 9. Southern India. 10. A lot of interior Australia.

Q2 **a)** …..deforestation….. **b)** Overgrazing……...soil erosion. **c)** ….there are then too many animals who overgraze and leave the ground bare leading to soil erosion. **d)** …..soils to become dry, loose, unprotected by vegetation and erosion occurs.

Q3 Correct statements are: Desertification is a problem in both MEDCs and LEDCs. It is very difficult to reverse the effects of desertification.

Q4 **a)** Soil erosion is the removal of soil by wind or rain, far faster than it can be re-formed. **b)** In both.

Q5 1) wind 2) rain.

Q6 **1.** Ploughing in lines up and down the slope causes rain to run down, carrying soil and eroding gullies (channels).
2. Deforestation on slopes leaves them unprotected from the rain, and also there are no longer any roots to hold the soil in place.
3. Overgrazing leaves the ground bare and unprotected from rain and wind.
4. Very large crop fields leave soil bare in winter, and easily eroded by wind in flat areas or rain on slopes.
5. Loss of hedgerows removes natural windbreaks leading to wind erosion. Also the roots no longer hold the soil.
6. Modern monoculture and chemicals do not let the soil recover its fertility, and also if all traces of the crop are removed, there is no dead matter to enrich the soil and hold it together, so that it becomes infertile and loose.

Pages 39 – 47

Q7 a) Nepal. b) The West of USA eg Oklahoma. c) Kenya (other possible answers are Ethiopia, or Sudan). d) Britain – East Anglia.

pages 40, 41

Q1 a) Primary industry is the obtaining of raw materials or resources from the earth, such as coal or wood.
b) coal mining; farming; forestry.
c) Fishing.
d) Raw Materials.

Q2 a) Secondary industry (manufacturing) is the making of things from the raw materials eg wheat is made into cakes, or iron is turned into steel for knives and forks.
b) 1) the manufacture of clothing 2) the making of furniture.

Q3 a) Tertiary industry is the name for services, where people are employed in doing a service for others, such as in a bank. They are not making products.
b) 1) nursing 2) travel agent 3) hairdresser. (lots of other possible answers here, such as teachers, doctors, police, the army)

Q4 a) Quaternary industry is the newest type of industry, involving modern technology. It is about researching into and developing new ideas eg in computers, and other forms of modern communication and science.
b) 1) computers 2) mobile phones.

Q5 a) Nepal is B; b) USA is A; c) Tertiary; Primary.

Q6 Inputs box: money (capital), sugar, flour.
Processes box: baking, kneading dough.
Outputs box: bread, cakes.
Feedback box: profits ploughed back into the firm.

Q7 a) Linkages describes how one industry relies on others. eg a firm that makes jam is linked to a glass manufacturer who supplies the jam jars, and to the sugar refinery for the sugar, and to a paper factory for the labels…..and to others…
b) The Car Industry is an assembly industry – it collects all the parts (components) from various suppliers and puts the finished cars together at an "assembly plant". This plant does not manufacture the various parts.
c) The car industry does not need to locate near raw materials – it can locate near a large workforce or near a large market, which is more efficient, and collect all the parts at this central location.
d) If a components firm goes out of business or is on strike, it will affect the car assembly firm.

pages 42–44

Q1 a) 3; b) 2; c) 4.
Q2 a) F; b) T; c) T; d) T; e) F; f) T.
Q3 Road - Adv: door to door service; convenient to use special container lorries. Disadv: traffic jams; costly.
Rail - Adv: cheaper; good for heavy bulky cargoes eg coal. Disadv: slower than road; goods have to be taken to and from railway stations by other means.
Ship - Adv: cheaper; good for some bulky cargo eg oil; grain. Disadv: slower; only for certain routes (overseas, or river/canal routes).
Air - Adv: fast; good for perishable goods eg exotic fruit and vegetables. Disadv: expensive; not suitable for heavy bulky goods.

Q4 The market is the area of people where the goods are sold. Eg Japanese cars are sold in the "European market", which means that they are sold in lots of countries in Europe.

Q5 1) Car assembly – reason is because finished cars are more difficult to transport, so it is better to assembly them near where they will be sold. 2) Food manufacture eg bread – reason is that these products are perishable and need to be sold fresh, so they need to be made near where they will be sold.

Q6 a) Industrial agglomeration is where there are lots of linked industrial firms concentrated in one area. Eg the West Midlands.
b) 1) Transport costs between firms are smaller. 2) The firms can share the labour force and the market of the area.
c) 1. Central Scotland (Clydeside); 2. NE England (Tyneside); 3. Lancashire and Yorkshire; 4. The Midlands; 5. South Wales; 6. The London area.

Q7 a) 1) Near to labour force. 2) Near the CBD which was the market. 3) Transport was limited so it was best to be near the city centre, and also the workers had to be within walking distance of the factory (cars only just being invented in the 19th century!)
b) Near the railway and the canal.
For the transport of heavy bulky goods.
c) On industrial estates near main roads.
Because there is much more space further out, and land was cheaper.
d) They are located out of town close to good transport links
1) These sites are more attractive (greener) than inner city ones;
2) There is much more space to build purpose-built buildings and car parks. 3) There is good road access, using motorways.
e) 1) To provide employment for the many unemployed people who live there.
2) To reduce damage to the environment in the Green Belt.
3) To slow down urban sprawl by using existing sites (called Brown Sites).

page 45

Q1 The Formal Sector is employment which is regular and people are paid a wage. Eg in a factory.

Q2 a) The Informal Sector is employment that people have created for themselves, and make a little money from time to time, such as carrying bags for tourists.
b) Because it provides jobs especially for the new migrants who arrive in the cities in great numbers. There are not enough formal jobs.
c) Because it is not regular, and so many people do not have a regular wage, and are therefore very poor.

Q3 FORMAL – olive oil manufacturing; pottery; soft drinks; leather tanning, bags.
INFORMAL – sewing and shoe repairs; selling snacks; tourist guides; car washing.

Q4 Hours are longer, and wages are lower, than in MEDCs.

Q5 1) They do not have enough money to invest in industry.
2) Many LEDCs' infrastructure (roads, railways, services) are poorly developed which makes the development of industry difficult.

pages 46, 47

Q1 Newly Industrialised or Industrialising Country.

Q2 Pacific Rim; South Korea; Taiwan; Hong Kong; Singapore; Tigers; United States; Britain.

Q3 a) The NICs have large populations, providing the countries with a large pool of cheap, hard working labour. b) The Governments give strong support (grants, training programmes, and control of imports and exports), and they have invested a lot of the profits into new roads, railways, airports, buildings such as schools and colleges. c) There is a huge market for the NICs in Asia eg China. d) Large MNCs like Sony have invested money in the NICs, and set up factories using their cheaper labour. e) The NICs have been very successful due to the leadership of very good businessmen who own the large family businesses eg in S Korea – Daewoo, Hyundai and Samsung.

Q4 a) A third. b) It had decreased to about a sixth of the total. c) It doubled. d) The % in services is very similar, although there was a slight increase by 1991.

Pages 47 – 55

e) 1) banking 2) transport. (other possible answers include teaching, nursing, insurance).

Q5 Raw materials.

page 48, 49

Q1 **a)** Manufacturing. **b)** Numbers employed in manufacturing and services were the same. **c)** They fell to almost half of the 1971 figure. **d)** They rose.

Q2 **a)** 1) Foreign countries competing with our products forced some firms to decline. 2) Our manufacturing firms have become more mechanised, so that they need fewer workers. (Another reason is that there has been a huge expansion in certain services eg tourism and banking).
b) banks; doctors; teachers; solicitors; police.
c) 1) iron and steel; 2) shipbuilding; 3) cotton; 4) wool.
d) Your answer will be your local example. Eg in the West Midlands, there used to be a steel works which closed, and the site was re-developed as the Merry Hill Centre – a retail park.

Q3 1. Tertiary and Quaternary. 2. Secondary. 3. Primary.

Q4 Correct words are: north; steel; is not; imported; footloose; where they wish; roads; markets.

Q5 **a)** An area with an agglomeration of Hi-Tech industries, and modern research and development.
b) 1) Computers; 2) Televisions 3) Mobile Phones.
c) Tertiary.
d) 1) Near a skilled labour force; 2) A greenfield site with plenty of space for buildings and car parks; 3) Near Universities who are also doing the research. (Another important factor is near major roads).
e) Footloose. They haven't got any specific location restrictions so they can set up where the workforce is.

page 50

Q1 A very large company or business, with the headquarters in an MEDC such as USA, and with branch factories and businesses in a lot of other countries all over the world. They are very powerful and control a lot of world industry and trade.

Q2 **a)** Britain and Holland.
b) Because these countries have the money and the highly skilled and qualified labour force. Also they have the Science Parks and Universities doing the research.
c) A country in which the company sets up branch factories and production areas of raw materials eg crops.
d) India and Zaire. LEDCs. 1) The labour is plentiful and cheaper. 2) Their climate allows the growth of the crops which are the raw materials eg tea. 3) Their large populations make a large market for the products.

pages 51, 52

Q1 Sustainable Development meets the needs of today's population without harming the ability of future generations to meet their own needs. *(This means a way of developing which is environmentally friendly, and non-damaging to the planet. It includes the ideas of conservation.)*

Q2 **a)** These can be used but will not run out.
b) 1) Wind; 2) Water; 3) Solar power (or wave, geothermal, tidal, biomass).

Q3 **a)** These will run out; they cannot be formed at the speed at which they are being used. **b)** 1) coal; 2) oil; 3) metals.

Q4 **a)** Because they were formed a long time ago in Geological Time, eg coal is made of the remains of trees – it is fossilised wood.
b) 1) coal. 2) oil. 3) gas.
c) Acid rain and global warming

Q5 **a)** food and water. **b)** soil erosion and desertification. **c)** deforestation and flooding. **d)** habitats and eyesores.

Q6 **a)** 1) Because their populations are growing so fast, so that more and more fuel is needed. 2) Because these countries often have no or few other sources of fuel.
b) 1) soil erosion – loss of soil in the rain or wind, as the protection of trees has been lost. 2) increased run off when it rains, leading to landslides and floods.

Q7 **a)** Limestone. **b)** 1) Scarring – huge holes and piles of waste rock. 2) Noisy lorries. 3) Dust in the air. **c)** 1) Jobs. 2) Waste rock used to protect the coast from erosion. 3) Geology students can study in the quarries. **d)** They make good habitats for plants and wildlife.

Q8 **a)** 1) Double glaze the windows. 2) Insulate the loft. Both keep the heat in.
b) 1) Contour ploughing (ploughing round the slopes, not up and down). 2) Strip cropping (growing different types of crops in strips, so that the ground is always covered).

pages 53–54

Q1 **a)** wind power
b) exposed lowland coastal areas; fairly flat mountain tops.

Q2 **a)** uranium. **b)** small. **c)** 1) near water 2) remote place far from large centres of population.
d) Advantages: produce very small amounts of waste, one reactor produces a lot of energy, the nuclear industry provides employment, nuclear fuels produce less carbon dioxide and sulphur dioxide than coal or oil power stations.
Disadvantages: the waste is radioactive (dangerous), accidents like Chernobyl happen, leaks can contaminate the environment and harm wildlife and people.

Q3 1. A dam is built across a deep valley in an area of hard, impermeable rock. 2. The large, deep reservoir provides the "head" of water. The water pressure at the base of the dam is very high. 3. The water flows with great force through pipes to the power house. 4. The fast flowing water turns the turbines, to generate the electricity. 5. Electricity is taken to towns and industry using pylons.

Q4 **a)** This is energy from heat deep in the ground. Iceland is a volcanic area, and water percolating into the ground becomes hot as it comes into contact with magma – instant central heating!
b) Energy from biomass uses waste such as plant remains and animal manure, which produces heat and gas as it decomposes.
c) 1) The barrage would interrupt shipping routes. 2) It would disturb wildlife eg fish.

Q5 **a)** environment. **b)** technology. **c)** efficient.

Q6 1. Double or even triple glazing of windows to conserve heat.
2. Switching off lights in rooms not being used. (Other ideas could be the use of the special energy saving light bulbs, and appliances like energy-saving washing machines.)

page 55

Q1 Acid Rain is rainfall which is very acidic (it's pH is lower than normal rainfall).

Q2 1. Power stations burn coal, oil and gas, which release pollutants especially sulphur dioxide into the air, as gases and particles. Cars burn petrol and this releases nitrogen oxides into the air.
2. The pollution is blown in the winds, and carried for miles.
3. Sulphur dioxide combines with water in clouds to form weak sulphuric acid, and nitrogen oxides form nitric acid, to create acid rain. 4. The rain (and snow) that falls is more acidic than normal, and it kills trees and damages soil, water and buildings.

Q3 This is because the pollution is carried in the winds, far from the source of the pollution. The Westerly winds blow pollution from Canada to Britain, and from Britain to Scandinavia, where it mixes with the water vapour and rain to become acid rain.

Pages 55 – 63

Q4 a) Acid Rain kills leaves and makes the soil too acidic for the plants to live. b) The rivers and lakes become more and more acidic, so that plants and fish die. c) Soils become acidic; The acid water draining through the soil leaches the nutrients so that crop yields fall. d) The nutrients from c) end up in ditches and streams, making them nutrient-rich, (this is eutrophication), which causes an overgrowth of plants and algae. The decomposition of all this plant material as it dies causes the water to be starved of oxygen so that creatures die.

Q5 1. Power station chimneys can have devices called "scrubbers" fitted to them, extract some of the sulphur dioxide, reducing the pollution. 2. The use of alternative forms of energy like wind, solar and hydroelectric power do not cause pollution of the air, and therefore help to reduce acid rain formation. 3. If we reduce our use of cars, this will mean less pollution and less acid rain formation. One way is to increase the use of public transport, or use bicycles.

pages 56, 57

Q1 Global Warming is the slow rise that is occurring in the earth's average temperatures, due to human activities.

Q2 0.5 C.

Q3 1. The burning of the rain forest releases the gases carbon dioxide and methane into the air.
2. Cleared areas no longer use up the gas carbon dioxide in photosynthesis.
3. The burning of fossil fuels releases carbon dioxide into the air.
4. Cars burn fossil fuels too.
5. The sun's rays can pass through the atmosphere, and warm the earth.
6. But heat from earth cannot escape through the pollution, and so the temperature rises.

Q4 a) Greenhouse gases. b) These gases trap the heat which is going out from earth, and prevent it from escaping, which is what the glass does to heat inside a greenhouse. This is how a greenhouse stays warm. c) 1) Carbon Dioxide; 2) Methane. (There are others, eg Nitrous oxide, and CFC Chlorofluorocarbons.)
The gradual rise of average world temperatures

Q5 a) It is melting. b) Warmest. c) They are rising. d) 1) Melting ice; 2) Warmer sea water expands so sea levels rise. e) Most of the country will flood. f) 1) Holland; 2) SE England eg London; 3) The coast of East Anglia; 4) Islands like the Maldives will disappear. (Other answers possible eg Florida coast, Australia coast.)

Q6 a) There may be more destructive hurricanes.
b) 1) This will damage the tourism industry. 2) It will damage farming and buildings. c) It may become wetter, so that more farming can occur. d) Crop yields might fall, and grazing land might dry up. e) Harvests might be poor if the land becomes wet all the time due to flooding, and the floods may well be of sea water – too salty for crops. f) Food shortages, and famine.

pages 58, 59

Q1 Pollution is the damage to the environment.

Q2 The environment means the air, water (rivers, lakes, seas), land, and includes the scenery – which can be spoiled by ugly buildings.

Q3 a) Burning fossil fuels (coal, oil and gas) releases carbon dioxide, nitrogen oxides and sulphur dioxide into the air. b) Vehicles pollute the air – their exhausts give out nitrogen oxides, sulphur dioxide, carbon monoxide, and older ones give out lead too. c) Farm chemicals (pesticides and fertilisers) are sprayed and get into the air. d) Burning trees in the destruction of rain forests eg in Amazonia, and forest fires eg in Australia release the carbon which becomes carbon dioxide and methane.

Q4 1) Farming may pollute the river with fertilisers and pesticides eg around Orange. 2) Industrial waste and hot water may pollute the river, eg at Lyon. 3) Sewage may be discharged into the river – there are many towns eg Avignon. 4) Oil and litter from pleasure boats may pollute too eg Avignon.

Q5 a) ——The coast of North East England. b) ——The Exxon Valdez, Alaska, 1989. c) ——The Mediterranean Sea.

Q6 a) matches up with 2); b) matches up with 1); c) matches up with 4); d) matches up with 3).

Q7 1) In housing areas near airports. 2) In housing areas near motorways.

Q8 a) Visual pollution. b) Thermal pollution.

Q9 a) Eutrophication is the process of making streams and ditches too rich in nutrients, so that there is a lot of growth of plants and algae. The nutrients come from fertilisers from the fields nearby.
b) 1. Rain falls on crop fields and leaches the fertilisers (nitrates) and they drain into the stream. 2. Some of the rain runs off the fields, taking fertiliser into the stream. 3. In the streams, the levels of nutrients increase – this is eutrophication - and this causes weeds, plants and algae to grow too much. 4. The water becomes starved of oxygen because this is used up during the decomposition of all the plants as they die, and this causes other life to die, eg fish.

pages 60, 61

Q1 A National Park is an area of outstanding natural beauty eg mountains or lakes. The area is protected so that the public can enjoy the scenery.

Q2 a) The National Park Authority. b) 1) …..environment. 2) ..enjoyment ….understanding… 3)….residents. c) It is difficult to protect the environment when the area has so many visitors every year. Also people live there, and the residents may be disturbed by the cars and coaches of the visiting tourists. Residents need houses and jobs which may affect the scenery. d) Conflicts.
e) Since 1951, more and more people have acquired a car, so that the Parks have become much more accessible. Also there are more coach tours, faster trains, and faster roads (there were no motorways in 1951). f) Problems have resulted such as noise, pollution, overcrowding, parking problems, damage to footpaths, litter.

Q3 a) moorland; b) about ½; c) farming; d) 1/3; e) 1/6; f) 1) lakes 2) buildings.

Q4 a) no; b) yes; c) yes; d) no; e) yes; f) no.

Q5 Reading the rows horizontally: Farming – no conflict with Forestry; conflict with walkers (who leave gates open, and litter, and dogs scare animals), cars and coaches (noise, fumes). Forestry – conflict with walkers, cars, coaches (danger during tree felling). Walkers – conflict with cars and coaches (danger, noise, pollution). Days out by car – conflict with coaches (busy roads, parking problems, fumes).

Q6 a) Carlisle and Penrith; Newcastle and Durham; Leeds and Sheffield; Birmingham. b) 8 million. c) 1) walking; 2) shopping; or visiting interesting limestone scenery. d) 1) People leave litter which looks ugly and can be a hazard to animals. 2)Walkers and climbers in large numbers erode the paths or Large numbers of cars and coaches cause noise, air pollution and car parks have to be built. e) 1) One way would be to have park and ride schemes, so that people have to leave their car on the edge of the Park. 2) Another way could be to make the car parks very expensive and encourage visitors to use buses or bikes.

pages 62, 63

Q1 Human – museums; art galleries; restaurants; churches; famous buildings. Physical – hot sunshine; snow; waterfalls; wildlife; beaches.

Q2 a) London; b) Switzerland; c) Kenya; d) The Bahamas.

Section Seven — Answers

Pages 62 – 72

Q3 a) But conservationists say that roads create danger, noise, and pollution; the building of toilets and cafes can be an eyesore, with litter and waste disposal problems; car parks destroy habitats and cause noise and pollution. b) But residents say that they need jobs eg in the limestone quarries, and they need houses and new shops – so these cannot be kept out of attractive areas. c) But farmers say that tourists cause damage to stiles and walls, trample paths, leave litter, leave gates open so that animals get out, and their dogs can worry animals. d) But walkers and fishermen want peace and quiet, and these noisy activities spoil their enjoyment of the areas.

Q4 1. Local farmers need more land, and may take over wildlife habitats. 2. Wildlife may destroy crops in their grazing. 3. Farmland is destroyed by the building of hotels and golf courses.

Q5 1. Dress – Women tourists dressed in swimwear or shorts and tee shirts can offend the people of many cultures, especially those where woman have to keep covered up in long robes.
2. Behaviour – Western tourists often behave in a different way to local people, eg locals may not be allowed alcohol; they may not be used to noisy behaviour late at night.

Q6 a) T; b) F; c) F; d) T; e) F.

page 64

Q1 a) 1) The building of hotels has destroyed sand dunes and seashore habitats. 2) Sea and rivers now polluted with sewage from hotels. 3) Water polluted by oil from boats. 4) Hotels use so much water that there are shortages. 5) Rubbish from hotels tipped near villages. (Another possible answer - building of multi-storey hotels spoils the lovely views along the coastline.) b) 1) Fishermen have lost their access to the beach because of the hotels. 2) Local farmers have lost land as golf courses have been created. 3) Local people's water is being used up because hotels use so much. 4) Hotel rubbish creates health hazard and smell because it is left near villages. c) They go abroad, to the foreign companies. d) This is a problem to Goa because the wealth from tourism could be very useful to the local area and to India. It could help to create schools, roads, clinics etc. e) Correct word to circle is EXPLOITATION.

page 65

Q1 a) Gross Domestic Product per head (per person) — the total value of goods and services produced in a year per head. b) Gross National Product — A similar measurement but including invisible earnings like foreign investments. c) How long a person can, on average, expect to live. d) The number of babies who die before reaching the age of one, per thousand live births.

Q2 Literacy Rates – the percentage of adults who can read enough to get by. (Other answers are possible eg Energy consumption, number of people per doctor)

Q3 a) A scatter graph. b) LEDCs. c) MEDCs. d) B. e) The graph shows that in wealthier countries like Britain, there are fewer people per doctor, which means that there is a better health service. In a poor country, there may be hundreds of people over a large area with only one doctor. f) Negative – as wealth decreases, the number of people per doctor increases.

pages 66, 67

Q1 a) USA, Australia, Britain. b) MEDCs. c) More Economically Developed Countries, Less Economically Developed Countries. d) 1) The Third World 2) The Developing World.

Q2 C.

Q3 ..standard of living……primary, secondary, tertiary, or quaternary…….transport, education, health and leisure.

Q4 a) NICs – the Newly Industrialising (Industrialised) Countries. b) 1) Taiwan 2) Singapore (other answers possible eg Hong Kong, Malaysia).

Q5 a) This refers to the difference or contrast between the rich and poor countries. b) This is the line on a world map that separates rich from poor countries.

Q6 a)

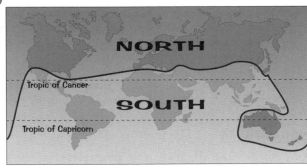

b) The Northern. c) 1) Australia 2) New Zealand.

page 68

Q1 a) climate. b) disease. c) pests. d) natural disasters.

Q2 a) Sudan. b) India. c) Nepal. d) Bangladesh. e) The Bahamas. f) Nigeria.

Q3 a) Malaria. b) Bilharzia c) Cholera (or Typhoid, or Dysentery)

page 69

Q1 a) Raw materials. b) For their industries eg cotton for the clothing industry. c) Manufactured goods. d) Because the price of manufactured goods is much higher than the price of raw materials. The MEDCs exploited the colonies, who had to supply them with cheap raw materials, and the MEDCs did not encourage the colonies to develop their own manufacturing industries. e) Because this would have caused competition with MEDC products. Also the MEDCs were becoming more wealthy by the colonial system. f) Dependency. g) An MNC is a Multinational Company, which is based in an MEDC and has branches in the LEDCs eg plantations which produce the raw materials.
h) 1) Unilever. 2) Britain and Holland. 3) Tanzania. 4) Margarine. (Other answers are possible eg 1) Dunlop, 2) Britain, 3) Malaysia, 4) rubber tyres.)

pages 70–72

Q1 …..exchange of goods and services …..

Q2 a) Imports are goods which are bought and received into countries from abroad. b) Exports are goods which are sent out of countries, to be sold abroad.

Q3 Raw materials.

Q4 1) cotton 2) rubber 3) tea 4) sugar cane. (Others are possible eg coffee.)

Q5 Manufactured goods.

Q6 1) cars 2) TVs 3) fertilisers 4) clothing. (Others are possible eg foods.)

Q7 The correct words are: lower; MEDCs; varies; rubber; cotton.

Q8 a) A is the price of manufactured goods, B is the price of raw materials. b) Manufactured goods. c) Raw materials. d) LEDCs don't know how much money they'll be earning from year to year, which makes planning for the future difficult. e) Through time, the 2 lines are moving further apart. This means that the difference in prices for raw materials and manufactured goods is getting bigger. It also means that the MEDCs are becoming richer, and the LEDCs are becoming poorer - the Development Gap is getting wider.

Q9 A Trade Bloc is a group of similar countries. They have joined together in trading agreements (making it an advantage to import and export within the group). a) EU – the European Union. OPEC – the Organisation of Petroleum Exporting Countries.

Section Seven — Answers

Pages 72 – 75

NAFTA – the North America Free Trade Association. **b)** They don't have charges (taxes or tariffs) on goods which they trade with each other, and they charge taxes on imports from outside the group, which makes these more expensive. **c)** The taxes on trade from countries outside the bloc are higher for manufactured goods than raw materials, which disadvantages the LEDCs. It makes it difficult for them to become industrial countries, and means that MEDCs can still buy their raw materials cheaply.

Q10 **a)** NICs – the Newly Industrialising (Industrialise**d**) Countries.
b) 1) South Korea 2) Taiwan 3) Hong Kong 4) Singapore.
c) 1) Trainers 2) cars. (Other answers are possible eg electronic goods.)

pages 73, 74

Q1 They need aid to help with development projects or emergencies. Aid can be money, goods, or services (eg technical staff, doctors).

Q2 LEDCs.

Q3 **a)** Aid given directly from one government to another. Eg money, food, rescue services, trained people. **b)** Aid is given to a central agency, eg the World Bank, who then distribute it. This is usually money. **c)** Aid given by organisations like Oxfam or the Red Cross eg help in disasters, or help for development schemes in villages. **d)** Aid which has conditions attached. Eg an MEDC lends money to an LEDC to buy fertilisers, but the LEDC has to agree to buy them from the lending country.

Q4 This answer will be your own case study of aid. It should look like this: In the Mozambique floods of February 2000, Britain sent aid, eg food, medical supplies, boats, helicopters, and trained staff such as doctors, and rescuers such as staff from the RNLI (Royal National Lifeboat Institution). Mozambique is one of the poorest countries of the world, and so much of the country's land and crops had been flooded, that they couldn't cope with the disaster themselves.

Q5 **The positives are:** 1) In disasters, aid saves lives and helps people in their stress eg Indian earthquake of 2001. 2) Aid for village projects like clean water supplies helps long term development and health. Eg the Blue Peter appeals on TV. 3) Aid for food production helps many LEDCs eg. The scientists of the MEDCs developed the new seeds and methods of the Green Revolution. 4) Aid in the form of medical training and education helps people's health and standards of living. Eg workers who go abroad in the VSO schemes – Voluntary Service Overseas. **The negatives are:** 1) Money aid makes LEDCs dependent and in debt – eg Brazil. 2) Aid money may be spent on large "prestige projects" such as irrigation, whilst neglecting the people who need more basic things like improved subsistence farming. Eg The Aswan dam in Egypt. 3) Aid given by MNCs for projects usually results in more profits for the MNC – Unilever has set up plantations and processing factories in LEDCs, but workers are paid low wages, and their products are sold cheaply to the company. 4) Aid doesn't always reach the people it is intended for – corruption occurs.

Q6 **a)** The best answer is 'C'.
b) I chose scheme 'C' because in the long term, these schemes will help the people to produce their own food, and they will not be in debt.
I did not choose 'A' because this could cause great debts.
I did not choose 'B' because MEDC-type of food is often unsuitable.
I did not choose 'D' because these large schemes are costly and often produce cash crops for export, and ignore subsistence crops. They can lead to debts.

page 75

Q1 Correct words are: the digging of a well; small; local people; the Government; self-sufficient.

Q2 Self-help schemes.

Q3 Appropriate technology.

Q4 **a)** …..clean water and sanitation schemes. **b)** ….clinic or a school. **c)** ….helping to set up cooperatives, to help people to borrow money or save it, which helps them to improve their farms and their standard of living.

Q5 **Advantages** …they can be for large-scale irrigation and farming, and provide water and HEP. They are "prestige or flagship" projects which make the country feel proud.
Disadvantages…They lead to debts; profits may go abroad to MNCs; the LEDC becomes dependent on the MEDC for skilled help; project may fail because the rest of the area is little developed (poor infrastructure); repairs difficult.

Section Seven — Answers